Seven Signs of the Second Coming of Christ

by Gary Frazier

Unless otherwise indicated, all Scripture quotations are taken from the New International Version of the Bible.

Seven Signs of the Second Coming of Christ

Published by Discovery Ministries
P.O. Box 13770
Arlington, Texas 76094
email: GDFRA77777@aol.com
website: www.discoveryministries.com

Printed in the United States of America

Library of Congress
Catalog Card Number: 99-60396
ISBN: 0-9653970-9-2

Dedication

This book is dedicated to my best friend and wife, Sandra, the greatest soul-winner and prayer warrior I have ever known, without whose constant encouragement, loving support and continuous prayers I could not have completed this endeavor. "A wife of noble character who can find? She is worth far more than rubies. Her husband has full confidence in her and lacks nothing of value. She brings him good, not harm, all the days of her life. Many women do noble things, but you surpass them all."

The Proverbs of King Solomon
Chapter 31, verses 10-12, 29

Contents

List of Illustrations

Preface

As we prepare to turn the calendar pages on a new millennium, expect a proliferation of prophets, soothsayers and "expert" commentators offering their take on the significance of this historic event. Myriad theories on the last days, Armageddon, the Second Coming of Christ and the rise of the new world powers are sure to abound. But for an accurate, up-to-date account of the times based solely on biblical truth, you would be hard pressed to find anything better than this work by my good friend Gary Frazier.

It is filled with facts not generally known regarding the nation of Israel, written by a man with unbounding love for that country. Dr. Frazier lives and breathes realized eschatology, and his assertions are based on a solid belief in the inerrancy of scripture, a deep love of Christ, and a passion for communicating both. His words are practical, sound and easy to grasp, yet they are filled with a sense of the early church's expectation of the return of our Lord — something we must recapture if we are to be true evangelists in these last days.

I recommend this book enthusiastically, and I urge its readers to study it carefully and apply its truth without hesitation.

Ed Young, Pastor
Second Baptist Church of Houston

Who Really Knows What the Future Holds?

"Tell us," they said, "when will this happen,
and what will be the sign of
your coming and of the end of the age?"
Matthew 24:3

Who knows what the future holds?

In 1956, self-proclaimed prophetess Jeanne Dixon contacted *Parade* magazine writer Jack Anderson. She told him that a Democrat would be elected president in 1960, but that he would die in office. That was the first inkling of her so-called famous prophecy. According to John Nebel, who hosted a radio talk show on WMCA in New York City, Jeanne Dixon was on his show January 23, 1963. She predicted on the radio before an audience of as many as 100,000 listeners that the president would be assassinated before the end of 1963. This "prophecy" called international attention to Ms. Dixon.

Yet the other prophecies Jeanne Dixon made in 1966 now look ridiculous. She foresaw that in the 1980s Red China would turn Africa and Asia against the United States, and this would lead to a world war. She prophesied that Russia would be the first nation to put a man on the moon. She also prophesied that Pope Paul VI would be the greatest Pope in Catholic history and that Richard M. Nixon would serve the country well. She further predicted the two-party system would vanish from the United States political scene.

Jeanne Dixon was wrong on every count!

Where do we find prophecy that is always and at all times accurate?

In the teens of this century, young Edgar Cayce, already thinking he possessed marvelous gifts, decided that in dreams he could diagnose ailments that orthodox doctors missed, and also prescribe treatments. He cured the daughter of the local school superintendent, who over the course of a year had become a vegetable. This event catapulted him toward worldwide fame.

Edgar Cayce had an uncanny knack for prediction. He not only foresaw the two world wars, but also picked the years they would begin and end. He saw the crash of the stock market in 1929 and the coming of the Great Depression. He also predicted its end in 1933. Before he died, he saw the collapse of communism in Russia and predicted in 1939 the deaths of two presidents while in office.

Yet Edgar Cayce also had colossal misses. He predicted that Hitler's motives were good. He further predicted that Los Angeles, San Francisco and New York would be destroyed within a period beginning in 1958 and ending with the millennium. These prophecies still await their fulfillment.

Yet where are the prophecies that without question are true and that give us firm ground for the future millennium?

In popular books and on television, the world has been virtually assaulted with the writings of Michel de Nostradame, who was born in 1503 in Saint Remi, France. We know him as Nostradamus. He wrote a series of four-line stanzas, collectively called the *Centuries*. There is virtually no event of this century that has not been claimed to have been predicted by Nostradamus. Yet when you read his prophecies they are uniformly vague and could be predictions of multiple events taking place in various centuries. Nostradamus leaves nothing but a puzzle.

In our world today, we are assaulted by voices from virtually every direction that seemingly know about our future. One need only turn on the television to hear of the self-proclaimed psychics spewing their offers of knowledge of the future. Prognosticators of the future have always been with us, even in ancient times. The only difference was that when a prophet of old prophesied, he was either 100% right or he was 100% dead. If he uttered a prophecy and that event did not occur, he was stoned to death. My how times have changed! Today we accept a self-proclaimed prophet if he or she is lucky and sometimes makes the right guess. Well, that old dog just won't hunt!

As I write these words, I am very near the site of one of the most significant and accurate prophecies in history. The apostle Peter wrote of this compellingly:

> *And we have the word of the prophets made more certain, and you will do well to pay attention to it, as to*

a light shining in a dark place, until the day dawns and the morning star rises in your hearts.

2 Peter 1:19

A more certain word

I am in Jerusalem, Israel, the most striking fulfillment of a prophecy in history. In A.D. 70, the prophecy of Jesus, that not one stone would be left on another at the site of the massive Temple of Herod the Great, literally came true. Since that time, Israel never became an independent state or the permanent home of any other people. It was conquered fourteen times in thirteen centuries. Yet over all those ages stood the promises of the Word of God. We may be certain that the God Who kept His promise concerning the return of Israel is the God Who will keep every other promise concerning the return of His Son, the Lord Jesus Christ, and the end of the world.

Jeanne Dixon was often wrong. Edgar Cayce was sometimes right, but then more than one spirit can animate prophecy. Nostradamus was so vague that his prophecies could refer to virtually anything. I am going to take you on a journey through prophecy, a journey that will take us through Seven Signs that speak to us of how close we are to the Second Coming of Christ. These signs are prophesied in the only accurate source in the world, the Word of God.

Signs speak to those who are listening

This book is about signs. Just as the hands of the clock inform us as to the chronological hour, these signs inform us as to what time it is historically and prophetically. People the world over and in all walks of life are seeking to know what time it is! They know time is running out. The sifting sand of the hourglass is sinking. The question, however, which longs to be answered is, "What does our future hold; what will the new millennium bring?" If time is running out for our world, for our existence in the world as we know it, then what does tomorrow hold? Most do not know that a more accurate question would be, "Who holds tomorrow?"

As I write these words, I believe with all my heart that we are living not just in the closing days of this millennium, but in the final days of our world as we know it! In fact, I feel as though we are on the sidelines hearing the countdown and watching the final seconds tick away!

I believe, based on a thorough study of the Word of God, coupled with an awareness of world events, that we are THE generation that will experience the coming of our Lord Jesus Christ for His Bride, the Church!

So, what time is it? It is time for the King to come again! We, who claim to know King Jesus, should be living with a heightened sense of expectancy, standing on our tiptoes in anticipation of His soon return. A great queen lived with that kind of expectation, even though her prince never returned. Queen Victoria became Queen of the British Empire on May 24, 1837, at the young age of 18. Incredibly, she reigned until her death on January 22, 1901. She was the Empress of the British Empire at the zenith of its power. Her beloved husband was Albert. Strangely enough, most remember Prince Albert more than Queen Victoria due to the advertising of Prince Albert tobacco. Perhaps you can recall, as I do, the childish prank in the fifties when a child would call on the phone and ask, "Do you have Prince Albert in a can?" If the reply was yes, they would then say, "Well, let him out, he can't breathe in there!" Prince Albert was the precious prince of Queen Victoria. Albert died December 14, 1861. For fifty years, Victoria was a widow. For fifty years, she dressed in black. For fifty years, she mourned the loss of her prince and longed for his return.

Donald Spoto, in his account of the House of Windsor, tells a remarkable story of what happened every day of those fifty years:

Every night at Windsor Castle the clothes of her beloved Prince Albert were laid out, freshly cleaned and pressed for the next day, as if she expected him to return on an excursion from Paradise, hoping to meet him in the corridors and go back with him to blessedness — a future which she believed in with all her being. And every morning fresh water was poured into Albert's bedside basin as if she could trick time into reverse.

What an incredible witness this is to the hope of a devoted wife for her husband, of a queen's love for her consort. We may well believe that the devoted Christian queen met her husband in glory in 1901. But she waited fifty years as the Widow of Windsor hoping that he would return, and he did not.

Millions of Christians are expecting the return of our beloved King, King Jesus, soon, in their lifetime. They are laying out the clothes in anticipation of the return of their king. Queen Victoria was disappointed that her prince did not return. With all my heart, soul and mind I believe this generation of born-again believers will not be disappointed. I believe we will meet King Jesus! Let us lay out the clothes and fill the basin. Jesus Christ, King of Kings and Lord of Lords is coming again soon. Maranatha, even so come Lord Jesus.

Christian leaders expect the coming of Christ soon

In recent months I have spoken to hundreds of respected ministers around America and have read numerous articles written by those who have expressed their belief in the soon-coming of Jesus. The general consensus among evangelical scholars is that things cannot continue on as they are and that the signs of His return are enveloping our world. Just listen to what a few of these Bible scholars are saying:

> *How are your bank accounts? They won't matter when He comes back. What about your long-range plans? They won't matter when He comes back. The Lord's return is so near. Long-range plans are foolish when there is so little time left.* [1]
>
> Henry Blackaby
> author of *Experiencing God,* December 7, 1997
> at First Baptist Church, Dallas, TX

> *One day in the not-too-distant future a King will come, the promised Messiah. Then Jew and Gentile alike will*

see Him walk upon the streets of Jerusalem. Together we will shout for joy as we look upon the King of Kings, and the Lord of Lords. [2]

John Hagee, Pastor
Cornerstone Church, San Antonio, TX

The signs of insecurity and shouts of revelation heard around the world are perhaps the death rattle of an end to an era in civilization . . . . The Scriptures promise that He (God) will act dramatically. He will send His Son back to earth.[3]

Billy Graham

The Lord is going to return. We need to get ready.[4]

Charles Swindoll

The hour hand on God's time clock is wound up and spinning. [5]

David Jeremiah

Dare we ignore the words of respected evangelical theologians? Can we afford to dismiss these warnings out of hand? I believe, as they, that if we do we will be as the people of Noah's day who ignored the warnings of the coming flood and as such our loss will be far greater, for that loss will be eternity!

The Bible promises the return of Jesus

Many people today are unaware of how much the Scriptures themselves speak of the return of Jesus Christ. Let me give you a brief overview that might surprise you:

1. *One out of every 30 verses in the Bible mentions the subject of Christ's return or the end of time.*
2. *In the 216 chapters in the New Testament, there are over 300 references to the return of Jesus.*
3. *Twenty-three of the 27 books of the New Testament mention Christ's return.*
4. *The Old Testament prophets, Job, Moses, David, Isaiah, Jeremiah, Daniel and most of the minor prophets, all spoke of the return of Christ.*

5 *Jesus Himself promised He would return.*

6 *The early church believed Jesus would return and taught this truth.*

The church through the ages taught Christ's return

The believers who followed the apostles clearly expressed their belief in the return of Jesus.

The Creed of Nicea: "… suffered and rose on the third day, ascended into heaven, and is coming to judge the living and the dead …"

The Nicene Creed: "… sitteth on the right hand of the Father and cometh again with glory to judge the living and the dead, of whose kingdom there shall be no end …"

The Athanasian Creed: "… Christ sat down at the right hand of the Father and is coming again with glory and power to judge the living and the dead."

The Articles of the Church of England: "He ascended into heaven and there sitteth until He returns to judge all men at the last day."

The Augsburg Confession: "… the same Christ shall openly come again to judge the earth according to the Apostle's Creed …"

The Apostles Creed: "… from thence He shall come to judge the quick and the dead."

All of the above have given testimony to believers' faith in the soon return of Jesus. If Jesus promised it … if the apostles believed it … if the early church taught it … if the church through the ages gave credence to it … if respected Bible scholars are warning us … then why won't we truly believe it?

Familiarity breeds indifference

Usually, when one approaches the subject of the soon-coming of Jesus Christ and the signs which Scripture says will precede this event, there are those who will counter with skepticism. Some of the most often heard arguments are:

It's been nearly 2,000 years and He hasn't come … every generation since Jesus has experienced numerous signs and there is still no return … no man knows the day or the hour when Jesus is coming back.

Each time I hear these weak and hollow-sounding arguments, I think about a phrase I heard years ago: Familiarity breeds indifference. With our 24-hour-news channels pouring the latest up-to-the-minute events into our homes and automobiles, our minds have become saturated with the evil of our world. We have become so familiar with violence that we no longer seem to be shocked when we hear of a teenager who stabs his mother to death and then proceeds to shoot his classmates at school, killing two and wounding many more. We have become so familiar with abortion we are no longer aghast when a teenage couple murder their just-birthed baby and dump the body into a trash can. The barrage of bad news heard daily causes us not to flinch when we learn of a mother who abandons her two small children in a car and pushes it into a lake, drowning both of them, or another who stabs her two children to death as they sleep serenely in their beds. The more we hear, the more we see, the more we are exposed, the more indifferent and passive we become! It seems that so many church folks have become so familiar with the teaching of the return of Jesus someday, that they cannot grasp the fact that someday is here! One cannot but help recall the words of the apostle Peter as recorded in 2 Peter 3:3, 4, 9, 10a:

> **3** *First of all, you must understand that in the last days scoffers will come, scoffing and following their own evil desires.* **4** *They will say, "Where is this 'coming' he promised? Ever since our fathers died, everything goes on as it has since the beginning of creation."* **9** *The Lord is not slow in keeping his promise, as some understand slowness. He is patient with you, not wanting anyone to perish, but everyone to come to repentance.* **10** *But the day of the Lord will come like a thief...*

We are warned in Scripture that there will be those who cast aspersions on the truth of the sooncoming of Jesus Christ. We are not to be surprised that many will turn a deaf ear to this timeless truth. The fact is, it is hard to believe the return of the King is going to occur any moment.

I am reminded of an old story my pastor and mentor, Dr. J. Frank Davis, told me many years ago. It seems one Sunday evening in a small rural church the pastor was preaching on the subject of the coming of Jesus.

At one point in his message he enthusiastically said, "I want everyone who wants to go to heaven to stand." Everyone in the small congregation leaped to their feet except one young boy seated on the very front row.

The pastor was so surprised by this that he looked at the lad and asked, "Son, don't you want to go to heaven someday?"

At that, the boy stood and said, "Yeah, someday! But the way you were talking, I thought you were getting up a bus load for tonight."

This seems to be the attitude of many today who believe King Jesus is coming again someday. They even want Him to come again someday. They just aren't sure they are ready for Him to come now. Once again, I believe someday is here!

The great deceiver

As believers, we agree that the Bible teaches that we have an enemy. Our enemy is none other than the devil himself, the fallen angel known as Lucifer. He is referred to numerous times in Scripture as the great deceiver. I know of no area of life where our enemy works harder than in the realm of the truth of the return of Jesus. His strategy is delay, procrastination. The lie he spreads is that Jesus is going to come again — SOMEDAY. However, we do not need to get in a hurry. There is no need to be zealous or concerned about this, after all it has been nearly 2,000 years. The result is that many have believed this lie. We can say that the consequence is that a great host of believers have become complacent and indifferent toward the coming of Jesus. Perhaps the greatest danger we face is that of believing half-truths. You may recall that when Jesus was tested by the devil in the wilderness, after having fasted forty days (Luke 4), it was the misquoting of Scripture or the misuse of Scripture which Satan used to try to deceive Jesus. The devil is not like Paul Harvey; he never tells the rest of the story!

The devil is afraid

The devil fears the believer who becomes convicted and convinced in his heart by the Holy Ghost that Jesus is coming soon, that time is running out. He knows that believer:

Will become a prayer warrior.

Will be bold in his witness for Jesus.

Will strive to live a holy life pleasing unto God.

Will see to it that every person he loves and cares about knows God loves him and proved it through the life, death and resurrection of Jesus.

Do you remember the story of the frog? You can take a frog and put him into a pot of boiling water and he will immediately leap out. However, if you put him in a pan of cool water on the stove, and turn up the temperature a degree or two at a time, he will sit there and be boiled to death. So it is with our enemy the devil. He is sly. He will never tell us that Jesus is never coming again. Rather he whispers, "someday, someday," and boils away our sense of urgency into one of indifference, one degree at a time.

Each summer, when I was growing up in Texas, my family took a vacation. My parents saved their money all year, and each summer we children looked with great anticipation to where we would go for those two exciting weeks. One summer we headed west to New Mexico and Carlsbad Caverns. I will never forget seeing those ancient caverns for the first time. I was so amazed by the great stalactites that hung down from the ceiling and the stalagmites that grew up from the floor! I remember vividly how the guide told us of their formation and how they did not appear at full size. Rather, they grew one mineral laden drop of water at a time over thousands of years. The devil hardens our hearts in the same way. He puts another layer of film over our spiritual eyes, another layer of wax in our spiritual ears and another fold of insensibility around our spiritual heart. His desire is to keep the believer looking every direction except forward to the coming of the King. He gets us to look backward to the way things used to be. He makes us look sideward at other people. He makes us look downward in depression and despair. He will even encourage us to look upward in prayer. Anything but forward to the coming of King Jesus. What direction are you looking these days?

Clarifying the coming:
Rapture or Second Coming?

One often hears of the coming of Jesus; but what is really being spoken of? It appears that so many today have failed to teach what the Bible teaches, and instead distort the teaching of the return of Jesus with its two phases. The Bible clearly teaches there will be two distinctively different future comings of

Christ. One will be the coming of Christ *for* the saints. The other will be the coming of Christ *with* the saints. Tragically, many believers have missed the distinction between these two separate events, and therefore are often confused as to the order of God's plan for Christ's return.

The coming of Christ for the saints

The last night of Jesus' life upon earth, prior to the crucifixion, was spent with His disciples in the Upper Room. They had gathered in Jerusalem to celebrate the Passover and its accompanying meal. After the meal, Jesus began to inform his followers of His soon departure and He said:

> *Do not let your hearts be troubled. Trust in God; trust also in me. In my Father's house are many rooms; if it were not so, I would have told you. I am going there to prepare a place for you. And if I go and prepare a place for you, I will come back and take you to be with me that you also may be where I am.*
>
> John 14:1-3

The words of Jesus were to those who had committed themselves to Him. We can safely apply these words to all believers through the ages. They had abandoned everything to follow Him. To this group He said He was going away. However, while He is gone He will not be idle, but rather He will be preparing a place, a home.

The setting speaks of the Jewish wedding ceremony. Without understanding the ancient rituals, one cannot grasp the portent of Christ's words. In ancient times marriages were arranged. Once the details of the marriage had been worked out, the couple was officially betrothed or engaged. However, betrothal was unlike our engagements in the sense that it was far more binding. It was in fact a legal bond and could only be terminated by divorce. Once the betrothal took place, the couple would return to their respective homes to prepare themselves for the wedding. The groom had to prepare a place, a home, for his soon-to-be-bride under the watchful supervision of his father. It was the father who would make the final determination as to the actual time of the wedding. This decision would not be made until he was satisfied that the home was ready and the time was right. Meanwhile, the bride was to be preparing herself. She was to be readying her belongings, but most importantly, watching, waiting and listening. She, like her groom, did not know the exact day or hour when her groom was going to return for her. Therefore she was to be in a state of constant readiness. Likewise, Jesus was teaching His followers that this was the way it was going to be regarding His return. Once His heavenly Father determined everything was ready and the time was right, He would return and claim His bride. This return, however, would be ONLY for His bride, the church, those who had truly committed themselves to Him by faith. Hence, Jesus spoke the words in Matthew 24:36, *"No one knows about that day or hour, not even the angels in heaven, nor the Son, but only the Father."*

The apostle Paul understood this great truth. In his letter to the believers in Thessalonica he proclaimed:

For the Lord himself will come down from heaven, with a loud command, with the voice of the archangel and with the trumpet call of God, and the dead in Christ will rise first. After that, we who are still alive and are left will be caught up together with them in the clouds to meet the Lord in the air. And so we will be with the Lord forever. Therefore encourage each other with these words.

1 Thessalonians 4:16-18

The great missionary apostle also wrote to the believers in Corinth and stated:

Listen, I tell you a mystery: We will not all sleep, but we will all be changed—in a flash, in the twinkling of an eye, at the last trumpet. For the trumpet will sound, the dead will be raised imperishable, and we will be changed. For the perishable must clothe itself with the imperishable, and the mortal with immortality.

1 Corinthians 15:51-53

John, the beloved apostle, banished to the Isle of

Patmos recounts:

> *After this I looked, and there before me was a door standing open in heaven. And the voice I had first heard speaking to me like a trumpet said, "Come up here, and I will show you what must take place after this."*
>
> Revelation 4:1

Three truths concerning the Rapture

There are at least three truths we glean from the teachings of Jesus, Paul and John. This coming of Christ for the saints will be:

Selective: He is coming only for His bride, the saved in and out of every denomination.

Sudden: He is coming at a previously unknown moment. No one knows the precise day or hour but God in heaven.

Silent: The world will neither hear nor see Jesus; only His own, His bride, will hear the trumpet blast and see Him as He appears in the sky. He calls us up to meet Him in the air.

If you are a student of Scripture, you will

recognize this as the event many refer to as "The Rapture of the Church." Although the word *rapture* does not appear in the Scriptures themselves, the concept is clearly taught. The Greek word in the original language of the New Testament, *harpazo*, means "to seize" or "to snatch up." The word "rapture" itself comes from the Latin translation of the Bible known as the Latin Vulgate. In the Latin Vulgate, we find the word *rapti*, hence the word rapture.

I am aware there are those who have differing understandings of end-time teachings. In this discussion, however, I will not take the time to delve into the various eschatological positions. I choose rather to write based upon my own research and understanding. In addition, there are numerous excellent books which would help clarify these truths to the serious seeker.

The coming of Christ with the saints

The Scriptures teach us that following the departure

from earth of all believers, the world will endure a time of great tribulation. The interested need only read the accounts of Matthew 24:15-31 and Revelation 6-19:11 to see clearly the horrific events of this particular seven-year period. At the end of this Time of Tribulation, Scripture reveals the Second Coming of Christ to the earth. This is how the ancient prophet Zechariah describes it:

> *On that day his feet will stand on the Mount of Olives, east of Jerusalem, and the Mount of Olives will be split in two from east to west, forming a great valley . . . Then the LORD my God will come, and all the holy ones with him.*
>
> Zechariah 14:4, 5

Once again John, in the Revelation, beholds:

> *I saw heaven standing open and there before me was a white horse, whose rider is called Faithful and True. With justice he judges and makes war. His eyes are like blazing fire, and on his head are many crowns. He has a name written on him that no one knows*

but he himself. He is dressed in a robe dipped in blood, and his name is the Word of God. The armies of heaven (all believers raptured away previously) *were following him, riding on white horses and dressed in fine linen, white and clean.*

Revelation 19:11-14

Three truths of the Second Coming

Predictible: Will follow seven years of unparalleled tribulation.

Precise: Jesus will return to the Mount of Olives from which He ascended.

Public: The entire world will see Him.

It becomes crystal clear to the Bible student that the Scriptures teach two separate comings, or returns, of Christ. This becomes extremely important in one's understanding and application of events which indicate where we are in prophecy. (*See illustration 1 on facing page.*)

So, which coming?

While Scripture teaches that there are signs which

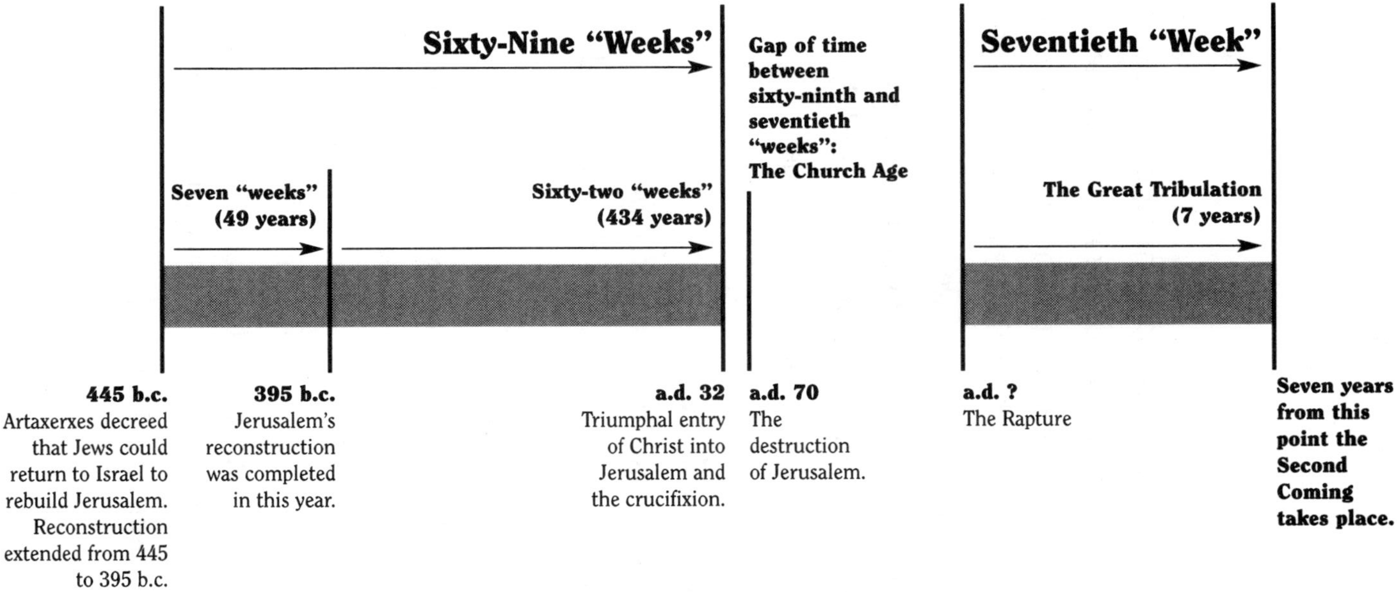

The Seventy "Weeks" of Daniel

"Seventy 'sevens' are decreed for your people and your holy city to finish transgression, to put an end to sin, to atone for wickedness, to bring in everlasting righteousness, to seal up vision and prophecy and to anoint the most holy. Know and understand this: From the issuing of the decree to restore and rebuild Jerusalem until the Anointed One, the ruler, comes, there will be seven 'sevens,' and sixty-two 'sevens.' It will be rebuilt with streets and a trench, but in times of trouble. After the sixty-two 'sevens,' the Anointed One will be cut off and will have nothing. The people of the ruler who will come will destroy the city and the sanctuary. The end will come like a flood: War will continue until the end, and desolations have been decreed. He will confirm a covenant with many for one 'seven.' In the middle of the 'seven' he will put an end to sacrifice and offering. And on a wing of the temple he will set up an abomination that causes desolation, until the end that is decreed is poured out on him."

Daniel 9:24-27

will forewarn us of the Second Coming of Christ, there are no signs which precede the Rapture of the Saints. The next event on God's prophetic calendar is the Rapture, the coming of Christ for the Saints.

One must understand this. If we have numerous signs which shout Jesus' Second Coming, then we are even closer to the Rapture of all believers! Are you ready, the groom is coming for His bride!

Weatherwise but otherwise

From before the days of the *Farmer's Almanac,* people have made weather proverbs. The old sailors used to say:

Moon clear at night, sailor's delight.

Moon red in the morning, sailor's sure warning.

As I write this, most of the country is under a threatening haze because of fires burning out of control in Mexico and Central America. People are able to look at the skies and predict what will happen because of the weather. With the Weather Channel, 1-900 weather numbers and talk radio, our generation knows more about the weather than ever before. You can even get computerized weather analysis and maps via the Internet updated hourly. Yet with all this information about weather, including advanced Doppler Radar and early warning systems of various kinds, the winter of '97 and the spring of '98 have been the most destructive in American history. The weather phenomenon known as El Niño swept across America wreaking havoc. Even though Americans were warned of the coming effects El Niño would bring, the warnings went unheeded. I recall tuning into CNN one evening in the late spring of 1998 to see the destruction from a storm on the west coast. One man being interviewed, whose home was devastated by the surging waters said, "I didn't really believe in El Niño until now." Unfortunately for him it was too late!

What about our generation? Are we missing the signs, the warnings that really matter? Are we heeding the words of the ancient prophets, of Jesus and of respected Christian leaders? Let's consider the generation of Jesus to see if we can glean something of value from His warning to them.

> *The Pharisees and Sadducees came to Jesus and tested him by asking him to show them a sign from heaven. He replied, "When evening comes, you say, 'It will be fair weather, for the sky is red,' and in the morning, 'Today it will be stormy, for the sky is red and overcast.' You know how to interpret the appearance of the sky, but you cannot interpret the signs of the times."*
>
> Matthew 16:1-3

In this passage, Jesus had an encounter with the Pharisees and Sadducees. The issue is whether or not He is who He says He is. Now remember it was the Pharisees and Sadducees who had the responsibility to teach the people the Word of God. They were supposed to be the spiritual leaders of this time. They came to Jesus and said, "If you are who you say you are, then prove it by giving us a sign from heaven." Jesus responded to their challenge with a very strong rebuke! He tells them they are better at forecasting the weather than they are at knowing what time it is, prophetically speaking!

It did not take a great deal of discernment to forecast the weather in first century Israel. The land was bounded by desert on the east and south, an ocean on the west and the mountains of Lebanon to the north. When the wind was blowing from the desert it would be hot. When the wind blew in from the Mediterranean, it would rain. Yet these religious leaders prided and plumed themselves on knowing the physical weather when they did not understand the spiritual temperature of their own times. John the Baptist, predicted by the Old Testament prophets, had come and gone. The Messiah of prophetic expectation stood in their midst. They recognized neither.

The Bible tells us God knows the heart of every man, and that God will never improperly judge a person. Having said this, we can then say that Jesus' rebuke of these religious leaders was justified because they could have and should have known He was who He said He was! How were they to know?

605 B.C. — God's alarm clock is set for the ages

Do you recall the events of 605 B.C. from your study of the Bible and world history? Nebuchadnezzar attacked the city of Jerusalem and carried captive to Babylon many of the people. In that group were some of Israel's brightest young men. One of those was Daniel, probably in his late teens at that time. Sixty-nine years went by, and in the year 537 B.C., God gave Daniel a dream, or vision. In this vision Daniel saw a panoramic view of the end of the world beginning from his very time:

> *"Seventy 'sevens' are decreed for your people and your holy city to finish transgression, to put an end to sin, to atone for wickedness, to bring in everlasting righteousness, to seal up vision and prophecy and to anoint the most holy. Know and understand this: From the issuing of the decree to restore and rebuild Jerusalem until the Anointed One, the ruler,*

comes, there will be seven 'sevens,' and sixty-two 'sevens.' It will be rebuilt with streets and a trench, but in times of trouble. After the sixty-two 'sevens,' the Anointed One will be cut off and will have nothing. The people of the ruler who will come will destroy the city and the sanctuary. The end will come like a flood: War will continue until the end, and desolations have been decreed. He will confirm a covenant with many for one 'seven.' In the middle of the 'seven' he will put an end to sacrifice and offering. And on a wing of the temple he will set up an abomination that causes desolation, until the end that is decreed is poured out on him."

Daniel 9:24-27

God's numbers: 7 + 62 + 1

God showed Daniel that the remaining days revolved around a time period of seventy sevens, some translations say weeks. The Hebrew word is *heptad* and it means weeks or a period of seven something, either days, weeks, months or years. From a careful study of supporting Scripture and history, we know Daniel wrote of a period of seventy times seven, or 490 weeks of years. By the way, this figure of seventy times seven or 490 is not incidental. The Jewish nation inhabited the land for 490 years. They were told to allow the land to rest every seventh year. It was to be a Sabbatical year of rest for the land (Leviticus 25:1-7). However, for seventy cycles of seven years they failed to heed God's command. As a result of their disobedience, God told them through the prophet Jeremiah, that if they would not allow the land to rest, he would take them out of the land and he would give the land the rest he had decreed. Judah went into captivity in Babylon for seventy years and the land rested (Jeremiah 25:11ff). Daniel knew and understood this from his personal study of Scripture.

God then showed Daniel in a dream that from the issuing of a decree to restore and rebuild Jerusalem, the remaining history of the world would progress through four periods of time.

The first period would be from the issuance of the decree forward seven sevens or forty-nine years. During this period Jerusalem would be rebuilt. You can read the remarkable story of the rebuilding of Jerusalem in Nehemiah chapters 1-3.

The second period, taking into consideration the seven sevens from the first period, would be from the decree forward seven sevens plus an additional sixty-two sevens, or 434 years. Do your arithmetic. You will find that when you add 49 years, plus 434 years, that you reach a total of 483 years. At the end of the 483 years the Messiah will be cut off or put to death. The Jewish people used the lunar calendar of 360 days in a year. 360 days multiplied by 483 years totals 173,880 days. (*See illustration 1 on page 31.*)

There was just such a decree issued by Artaxerxes, ruler of the Persians, on March 14, 445 B.C.! 173,880 days from that date in history leads one to the date of April 6, A.D. 32. It was the day Jesus mounted a young donkey in the village of Bethany and made His Triumphant Entry into

Jerusalem with the crowds going before Him shouting, *"Hosanna, Hosanna, blessed is he who comes in the name of the Lord"* (Matthew 21:9). It is the day known the world over as Palm Sunday.

Consider this. The Pharisees and the Sadducees knew the prophecies of Daniel and they could count! As a result of this, Jesus rightly rebuked them for failing to recognize who He was! In fact, I believe they did know who Jesus was but did not like what He was! (See John 11:45-53.)

Based on the above facts, let me pose a question. If Jesus rebuked the religious leaders of His day for failing to know what time it was prophetically, for ignoring the clear teaching of the Word of God ... how much more so would He rebuke us today? We have had 4,000 years of recorded history. We can look back historically to see the Word of God literally fulfilled time after time after time!

The third period revealed to Daniel is the period between the cutting off, or death of the Messiah, and the beginning of the final week of years. Remember there are to be seventy sevens. Jesus died after sixty-nine sevens so we are now in a gap, a parenthesis, between the end of the 69th week and the beginning of the 70th week. This span of time we call the Church Age. This gap has lasted nearly 2,000 years. This time period will come to an end with the Rapture of the Church, the coming of Jesus for His bride!

The fourth and final period begins with the signing of a covenant, or peace treaty between the nation of Israel and the coming antichrist who will rule the European Union (Daniel 9:27). This final week or seven years is known as the Trial and Tribulation Period or the Time of Jacob's Trouble (Jeremiah 30:7). This period will culminate with the Second Coming of Christ in power and glory to close human history as we know it! This event takes place exactly 2,520 days or seven years, from the signing of the peace treaty between Israel and the antichrist, leader of the one world government (Daniel 12:11).

God has a plan and it is not secret! God told Daniel:

But you, Daniel, close up and seal the words of the

scroll until the time of the end. Many will go here and there to increase knowledge.

Daniel 12:4

The word "knowledge" here is the Hebrew word *daath*, from the root word *yada*. It can and is often translated as "understanding."

In other words, God said that in the final days people will go to and fro in the word of God seeking to know prophetic truth and their understanding of it shall be increased. We are living in a time when we have the ability to comprehend and understand God's prophetic word unlike any generation that has ever lived. God wants us to know what time it is IF we are interested to know!

Do you want to know what time it is on God's clock? I can assure you that the hour is late. How close are we to His return? We are closer than we have ever been before! Our living Lord is returning.

During the great battles between the Spanish and the Moslem Moors, the hero of Spain was a daring soldier named El Cid. In a preliminary skirmish before the final great battle, he was gravely wounded. In fact, he died in the castle. The Spanish leaders were terrified that their soldiers' hearts would melt if they heard that their great general had died. So they did a deceptive thing. They placed his moribund body inside his full body armor and mounted him on his horse. They sent him through the gate of the castle. His astonished troops, knowing that he had been wounded, fell in behind him. They followed a dead leader on a white horse.

We are not deceived. We follow no dead Christ. When He returns, it will be a living Lord of history and eternity. Make sure you know what time it is on God's clock.

Signs of the Second Coming of Christ

Usually when someone speaks or writes on the subject of the signs of the times they are referring to Matthew Chapter 24 or parallel passages. In this insightful teaching of Jesus known as the Mount Olivet Discourse, Jesus informs His disciples that in the coming days there will be deceivers (false messiahs), wars and rumors of wars, ethnic strife, famine, pestilences, and earthquakes. He then says, "*All these are the beginning of birth pains*" (Matthew 24:8).

It is true that these signs will visibly precede the coming of Christ. The problem is that every generation since Jesus has experienced these signs in varying degrees. Although, I might add, no generation has experienced them like this generation! Truly our days are as birth pains. The closer we get to His coming, the more frequent the signs and the greater the intensity!

When a man or woman of God stands and begins to proclaim the coming of Jesus based on these signs, the unsaved church member or the unregenerate person outside the family of God, rises up and retorts, "Yes, but every generation for 2,000 years has experienced these signs and still He has not come back . . . give me some new news!"

CNN, ABC, NBC, CBS, the FOX network and hundreds of other news organizations comb our globe 24 hours a day, seven days a week, 365 days a year in a never ending search for news. Yet, I wonder if they, or the majority of their recipients, realize the importance of what is taking place. I wonder if they grasp that they are reporting the very signs that will usher in the second coming of Jesus. Signs that have not and could not happen until this generation of economic unity, religious ecumenism and emerging technology. Signs that scream Jesus is coming at any moment! I believe there are Seven Signs which demand our attention and understanding.

Dr. Gary Frazier with Prime Minister Rabin in Jerusalem, July 1995

[1] Donald Spoto, *The Decline and Fall of the House of Windsor* (New York: Simon & Schuster, 1995) p. 97.
[2] John Hagee, *Final Dawn Over Jerusalem* (Nashville, TN:Thomas Nelson, 1998) forward p. ix.
[3] Billy Graham, *Ten Reasons Why Jesus Is Coming Soon* (Sisters, OR, 1998) p. 46.
[4] Charles Swindoll, ibid., p. 16.
[5] David Jeremiah, ibid., p. 177.

1
Sign One: The Rebirth of the Nation of Israel

For I will take you out of the nations;
I will gather you from all the countries
and bring you back into your own land,
Ezekiel 36:24

Just a few minutes before 4 p.m. on May 14, 1948, David Ben-Gurion drove down Rothschild Boulevard in Tel Aviv, Israel. It was a bright, warm May afternoon. The beauty of the day, however, paled into insignificance because the next few minutes would be, perhaps, the most important in the history of the world since the resurrection of Jesus Christ! Ben-Gurion stepped lively into the modern two-story building which housed an art museum. Some 400 individuals, comprised of Jewish religious and political leaders, as well as press representatives from all over the world, waited anxiously. Moments later, precisely at 4 p.m. local time, Ben-Gurion called the meeting to order. In a matter of seventeen minutes he read the Declaration of Independence of the new State of Israel, and for the first time since A.D. 135, there was a land called Israel in existence. The words of the prophet Isaiah had finally come to pass. Seven hundred forty years before the birth of Jesus, Isaiah spoke these words:

Who has ever heard of such a thing? Who has ever

seen such things? Can a country be born in a day or a nation be brought forth in a moment? Yet no sooner is Zion in labor than she gives birth to her children.

Isaiah 66:8

This was the day when God made good on His promise for the rebirth of the nation of Israel and its restoration to the promised land. However, to understand fully the importance of this day, we must go back in history for a brief review of why a promise for resurrection, rebirth and restoration was necessary.

Noah + Ark + Flood = Nothing

The Bible, in its creation account, tells us that God created the heavens and the earth, and that everything God created was declared to be good. God placed His new creation, man and woman, in a perfect environment. The early pages of the Genesis record tell how God came to the garden in the cool of the day. He walked with Adam and Eve and obviously enjoyed sweet fellowship for a time. Sin came into the world as the two chose to believe the lie of Satan that they could be like God. The result of their choice was separation from God, as God put them out of the beautiful, secure garden. As we continue to read Genesis, we find the record of how the ancient world was in the process of becoming populated through this couple. Then, in the sixth chapter of Genesis we read some rather shocking words:

> *The LORD was grieved that he had made man on the earth, and his heart was filled with pain. So the LORD said, "I will wipe mankind, whom I have created, from the face of the earth — men and animals, and creatures that move along the ground, and birds of the air—for I am grieved that I have made them." But Noah found favor in the eyes of the LORD.*
>
> Genesis 6:6-8

God described His creation as being inherently evil and determined to destroy every living thing He had created. Scripture says in verse 8, "But Noah found grace in the eyes of the Lord." Noah was a man described as being perfect. The word actually means righteous or blameless. In other words, Noah had a heart for God. God's decision was to spare Noah, his wife, their three sons and their wives, and the animals God would bring to them.

God instructed Noah to build an ark. This was to be the means by which God would preserve them during His destruction of the created order by water. Noah and his family came out of the ark one year and eleven days after the first rain began to fall.

One may consider this the second great attempt of the devil to obliterate God's plan for His chosen people. God hangs the heaviest weights on the thin wire of His providence. It is not without significance that God shut the door to the ark. This unilateral divine act shows God's intent to preserve His people.

The Tower of Confusion

God started over again with just eight people. Strange as it was, after a relatively short period of time, man was back to his old ways again. This time, we find him in a plain in the land of Shinar (Gen. 11:2), in the region of ancient Mesopotamia. He has decided he can reach into heaven and be as God by building a great tower that we know as the Tower of Babel. God responds by confusing their language and scattering the people into different regions upon the earth.

Yet God again persevered in the preservation of His people and His plan for the creation of Israel. It is worth noting that in the mighty day of Pentecost, God reversed the curse of Babel in the coming of the Holy Spirit. There he gathered together His people again speaking one language (Acts 2-3).

This event brings us to the twelfth chapter of Genesis.

God does a new thing

God, at this point, had decided to do a new thing. That is, He was going to bring a new people upon the face of the earth, a people who would worship and serve Him and Him alone. Enter Abram! God speaks to the heart of a man by the name of Abram who was from the region of Ur located in the Mesopotamian area which today is Iraq. Abram had moved north to a place called Haran and there God spoke to him:

> *The LORD had said to Abram, "Leave your country, your people and your father's household and go to the land I will show you. I will make you into a great nation and I will bless you; I will make your name great, and you will be a blessing. I will bless those who bless you, and whoever curses you I will curse; and all peoples on earth will be blessed through you." So Abram left, as the LORD had told him; and Lot went with him. Abram was seventy-five years old when he set out from Haran. He took his wife Sarai, his nephew Lot, all the possessions they had accumulated and the people they had acquired in Haran, and they set out for the land of Canaan, and they arrived there.*
>
> Genesis 12:1-5

We do not know how God spoke to Abram. Was it in

a dream by night, a vision by day, or in an audible voice? Was it in a growing sense of disgust with the pagan worship of the moon deities of Mesopotamia? God spoke.

A people, a place, a plan

God made certain promises to Abram and those promises had to do with a new people. This people would be as numerous as the stars in the sky and the sand upon the seashore, a people who would reside in a land that was going to be theirs by divine decree. God not only promised a people and a place, He had a plan!

God made His promises to Abram when Abram was seventy-five years old (Gen. 12:4). Eleven years passed and Abram and Sarai still did not have a child. In desperation Sarai presented a plan to Abram. He was to have sexual intercourse with her Egyptian servant girl, Hagar. Through Hagar they became parents of a son whom God said they were to name Ishmael. However, this was not God's plan nor was

Ishmael God's promised heir! In fact God reaffirmed His promise of a miracle child to Abram:

> *When Abram was ninety-nine years old, the LORD appeared to him and said, "I am God Almighty; walk before me and be blameless. I will confirm my covenant between me and you and will greatly increase your numbers." Abram fell facedown, and God said to him, "As for me, this is my covenant with you: You will be the father of many nations. No longer will you be called Abram; your name will be Abraham, for I have made you a father of many nations. I will make you very fruitful; I will make nations of you, and kings will come from you. I will establish my covenant as an everlasting covenant between me and you and your descendants after you for the generations to come, to be your God and the God of your descendants after you. The whole land of Canaan, where you are now an alien, I will give as an everlasting possession to you and your descendants after you; and I will be their God."*
>
> Genesis 17:1-8

God promised the people and the place, but what about the plan?

> *Then God said, "Yes, but your wife Sarah will bear you a son, and you will call him Isaac. I will establish my covenant with him as an everlasting covenant for his descendants after him."*
>
> Genesis 17:19

It is very important that we understand that until the birth of the child of promise, Isaac, there was no such people as the Jewish race. God miraculously brought Isaac into existence when Abram was 100 years old and Sarai was 90. Isaac was the first Jew ever born upon the earth. Apart from the intervention of God, he could not have been conceived since Sarai was postmenopausal. It was impossible! God was now ready to do His new thing with His new people. There were some basic purposes why God brought the Jewish people into existence. I will mention only three primary purposes.

Why the Jew?

First, God brought the Jewish people into existence because He wanted a people, a race, who would be holy in their living, unlike the Gentiles.

Second, God intended for the Jewish people to infect the world with monotheism, the worship of one true God, Jehovah.

Third, God wanted to bless the Jewish people and show the rest of the world what He could do through a group of people who were wholly committed to him.

Were God's purposes and plans fulfilled in the Jewish people? One only need read the pages of the Old Testament to see. The Jewish people individually, and as a nation collectively, failed to meet God's desire for them. First, they failed to be holy in their living. Second, they became idolatrous in their worship. As a result of their attitudes and actions, God could not bless them. God repeatedly sent prophets to them to warn them of impending suffering and servitude. The message of the ancient prophets was, "Repent or you will be carried into captivity."

The message went unheeded and judgment came: first, in the form of the Assyrians, then the Babylonians, followed by the Medes and Persians, the Greeks and finally, the Romans. Not only did God send them prophets to call them to repentance, He sent His only son, the Lord Jesus Christ himself. The result of the failure to heed the message of Jesus brought the worst of all persecutions, dispersion from the land. Because the Jewish people failed to return to the God who loved them and who had exhibited His love through the physical presence of Jesus, Israel's homeland was taken from the Jewish people.

The Jewish people were so dispersed in the several waves of the *Diaspora*, or dispersion, that Roman historians considered that there was not a place where the Jew could not be found.

The great cities of the world are all marked by landmarks. The House of Parliament and the Tower of Big Ben identifies London. The Eiffel Tower stands as a monument to Paris the world over. The Statue of Liberty reminds us of New York. The Golden Gate Bridge recalls San Francisco.

In Jesus' world the landmark of Jerusalem was the Temple. Josephus wrote of the striking beauty of the Temple. The Jewish historian mentioned the roof of heavy golden plates which at sunrise reflected back a fiery splendor so luminous that the spectator would turn away his eyes as if looking at the sun itself. At a distance, the whole Temple appeared as if it were a mountain of snow with golden pinnacles.

Thus it had been all the more striking when Jesus predicted the absolute and total destruction of that building:

> *Jesus left the temple and was walking away when his disciples came up to him to call his attention to its buildings. "Do you see all these things?" he asked. "I tell you the truth, not one stone here will be left on another; every one will be thrown down." As Jesus was sitting on the Mount of Olives, the disciples came to him privately. "Tell us," they said, "when will this happen, and what will be the sign of your coming and of the end of the age?"*
>
> Matthew 24:1-3

As Jesus was leaving Jerusalem to go back over the brook Kidron, his disciples begged him to take in the stunning panorama of the Temple complex. Before them the building rose in colonnades of dazzling Jerusalem limestone topped by a golden roof and pinnacles. The distance from the pinnacle to the bottom of the valley was a dizzying 1,000 feet. The mass of the Temple itself sat on the colossal Herodian stones that have impressed observers for 2,000 years. The Temple stood in majesty as if fresh from the mason's hand. Its very solidity seemed to protest against the words of doom that Jesus had spoken.

The Jews in the days of Jeremiah had come to believe in the inviolability of the Temple. They looked at it as if it were some kind of magical charm or talisman that would prevent the city from falling. Just as the Temple had fallen in the days of Jeremiah, so it would fall again.

Thirty-eight years after Jesus had spoken those words of prophecy, they were fulfilled in a most literal way. It was the ninth day of the Jewish month

Av, which corresponds to our July/August. Titus, son of the Roman Emperor Vespasian, and his Roman legion had encircled Jerusalem. The city was under siege. The Romans had been at war with the Jews since an uprising in Caesarea in A.D. 66, and finally were about to destroy their capital, Jerusalem. History records there were over one and one-quarter million people trapped inside the city dying of starvation, yet unwilling to surrender. They had come to Jerusalem to celebrate the Feast of Passover and were caught as the final battle had begun. The daily sacrifice had ceased twenty-one days prior and all that was left to do was wait. The Roman Legion had advanced to the outer edge of the Temple complex. Titus, the Roman general, gave strict orders not to destroy the Temple. After all, it was the most beautiful building in the Roman Empire. He repeatedly implored the Jewish defenders to surrender and spare their city and their Temple. But it was not to be. The words of Jesus, spoken from the Mount of Olives, rang true:

O Jerusalem, Jerusalem, you who kill the prophets and stone those sent to you, how often I have longed to gather your children together, as a hen gathers her chicks under her wings, but you were not willing. Look, your house is left to you desolate.

Matthew 23:37-38

Despite Titus' firm orders to the Roman centurions, the enraged soldiers threw torches into the Temple and within minutes the Temple was engulfed in flames.

The Jewish historian, Flavius Josephus, was an eyewitness to the destruction. He wrote that General Titus stood in the entrance to the Holy Place beating back his soldiers with his sword in a futile attempt to save at least the inner Temple from destruction. It is also reported that when flames reached the inner sanctuary of the Holy of Holies, Titus fell to his knees and cried out, "As God is my witness, this was not done by my order."

Neither Titus nor his soldiers knew they were

unconsciously fulfilling the very words of Jesus.

Jesus' prediction is even more arresting when you consider that the ancient temples of Karnak, Luxor and Athens still stand. I have vivid memories of walking through the temple at Karnak, standing adjacent to the Valley of the Kings and Queens, and looking at the columns engraved with hieroglyphics. This temple has been towering over the desert sands for ages. I remember ascending the acropolis of Athens to the Parthenon, the temple to Athena, and pondering with amazement that it has stood for 2,400 years. Yet not a single stone of Herod's Temple stands one on top of another, in exact fulfillment of Jesus' words.

The result of the total destruction of Jerusalem was a worldwide scattering of the Jewish people into virtually every country on the globe.

Two powerful words: "But God"

But God had spoken through the ancient prophets and promised a return to the land in the last days.

Almost every one of the prophets spoke of the day when God would regather the Jewish people from wherever they were and bring them back into their land. Hence, May 14, 1948, was the fulfillment of this promise.

What were the circumstances that led to the rebirth of Israel? Throughout the centuries Jewish people have been the target for various ideologies of hate. Everywhere the Jews have gone, they have ultimately become a hated and despised transient people. This hatred seemed to reach its pinnacle under the Third Reich led by Hitler. History records the mass murder of six million Jews under the Nazis of Germany. Out of the ashes of the Holocaust, the Jewish nation was reborn. But, to understand, we need to look back a little farther.

After the dispersion of the Jews in A.D. 70, there remained a small group of Jewish people in the land. Sixty-five years later in the years between A.D. 132-135, the Roman Emperor Hadrian was dealing with yet another revolt in Israel. The leader, a man by the name of Simon Bar Kochba, was hailed as the Messiah. The Jews, under Bar Kochba's leadership, were successful in repelling the Romans for two years. Finally, Hadrian came with a large army and attacked and destroyed Jerusalem. On this final day, strangely enough, the ninth of Av, the very same day the Temple had been destroyed in A.D. 70, the last great Jewish army of an independent Israel was slaughtered. The Roman historian, Dio Cassius, recorded that 580 thousand Jewish soldiers were killed by the sword and many more by fire and famine.

Following this destruction of Jerusalem, Hadrian vented his anger on the Jewish people. In an act of rebellion against the God of the Jews, Hadrian changed the name of Israel to *Syria Palestinia,* hence the name *Palestine*. He also changed the name of Jerusalem to *Aelia Capitalina*. In addition, he built a pagan temple to Venus on the site where the ancient Temple had stood. Finally, he ordered that no Jew could approach the city of Jerusalem under penalty of death.

The years passed and Israel became a barren and deserted land with no permanent residents. The powers came and went. Romans, Byzantines, Persians, Arab Moslems, Seljuks, Crusaders, Mamelukes, Turks and finally after World War I, the British. By the end of World War I, there were almost 50,000 Jews back in the land. By 1928, the number rose to 160,000, which was twenty percent of the total population. Much of the mid-part of the century witnessed the amazing exodus of Jewry from Europe and elsewhere in the return to the Promised Land. This was in the face of constant vacillation on the part of both the British and American governments. The Jews encountered quotas limiting their return and outright danger. Some boats with immigrants were torpedoed, some sent to the African Island of Mauritius, and others sunk. One disabled ship, the *Struma,* stranded in Istanbul, was towed out to sea where it exploded, killing all but one of the 769 refugees en route to Palestine. Nevertheless, at the end of World War II in 1945, there were about 600,000 Jews in Palestine.

What an incredible act of God this is. You cannot find the ancient neighbors of the Jews anywhere. Have you ever met a Moabite? Do you know any Hittites? Are there any tours to visit the Ammonites? Can you find the postal code of a single Edomite? No! These ancient peoples disappeared from history and from the face of the earth. Yet the Jews, just as God promised, returned to their land.

After World War II, David Ben-Gurion visited the Nazi death camps at Auschwitz and Belsen. The result was a desperate determination to establish a homeland for the Jewish people. The nations of the world seemed in agreement. The time had come. The time was right. The time was now! Their home was to be their ancient land, the land that was being called Palestine. On May 13, 1948, Chaim Weizmann notified President Harry Truman that the Jews of Palestine were determined to declare the existence of their new state on the next day. Although Truman's advisors wanted him to confer with England and France, Truman did not want to hesitate. He wanted to recognize the new nation of Israel. Only eleven minutes after the declaration by Israel, the United States recognized its existence.

At sunrise on May 14, the flag of Great Britain, the Union Jack, was hauled down from its staff over the Government House in Jerusalem. The presiding British High Commissioner, Sir Allen Gorden Cunningham, then left the Holy Land for the last time amidst a seventeen-gun salute. The thirty-three-year British rule had ended. At 4 p.m. that same day, Israel's Declaration of Independence was read.

I want to point out to the reader, who may be unfamiliar with certain historical events, something of enormous importance. The Palestinians, those wandering nomadic people who came from the peninsula of Saudia Arabia, were offered the opportunity in late 1947 to have their own state alongside Israel. They refused. They stated, to the contrary, that if the Jews proclaimed a state, they would finish what Hitler failed to do. They would drive the Jews into the Mediterranean. At the root of this lies the intolerance of the Moslem religion.

The fight for survival in the land now became a War for Independence. On May 15, 1948, Israel was invaded by Egypt, Jordan, Syria, Lebanon and contingents from Saudia Arabia and Iraq. This pitted some fifty-five million Arab Moslems against 64,000 Jews. The odds were incredible. A few weeks before the outbreak of the war, British Field Marshall Montgomery toured the area. He surmised Israel could not survive a full-scale onslaught from the Arabs and that it would take the Arabs only eight days to destroy the Jews. Israel was long, narrow and had over 600 miles of frontier land to defend on three sides, and her back was against the sea. At one point, Israel was only seven miles wide. It seemed impossible, "but God!"

God + 1 = Majority

The Arab Moslem soldiers outnumbered the Jews 40

to 1, in population, 100 to 1, in equipment, 1,000 to 1, and in area, 5,000 to 1. The plan of the allied Arab troops was simple: Egypt would attack from the south and make for Tel Aviv and Jerusalem. From the north, Lebanese, Syrian and Iraqi armies would sweep though Galilee and Haifa and head to Tel Aviv. Jordan would come from the east and drive through the West Bank to Jerusalem. To defend themselves the Jewish soldiers had 10,000 old Italian-made rifles with fifty rounds of ammunition each. Once fired, the barrel had to be submerged in a bucket of water to cool it down so that it could be reloaded. They had four ancient artillery pieces and 3,600 submachine guns. The situation seemed absolutely hopeless for Israel, "but God!" For the Arabs, this was a war of expansion. For the Jews, it was a war for survival! It is a known fact that human beings will fight harder to save their lives than to enlarge their lands. This, too, made a difference in the attitudes of the soldiers. Dr. G. F. Owens writes:

Four exceedingly important goals lay before the

Jewish military leaders: first, to defend to the utmost every Jewish settlement in the path of the invading armies; second, to create a navy to lift the blockade and bring in men, munitions, and immigrants by way of the sea; third, to lift the siege of Jerusalem; and fourth, to take the offensive and save Israel. [6]

Israel was successful in accomplishing all four goals and on February 24, 1949, the War for Independence came to an end.

Rabbi Abraham Joshua Heschel notes an even more miraculous truth about the Land of Promise across the centuries. Since the destruction of Jerusalem in A.D. 70, Israel never became an independent state or permanent home for any other people. It was conquered fourteen times in thirteen centuries. Each of the conquerors took it as an occupied territory to be ruled from outside. The odd conglomeration of residents was a hodgepodge of people forced to convert to Islam by the Moslems. Consider the situation:

Universal was the legacy of desolation. Most of the country had sunk back into the oblivion of swamp in the north and eroded soil and sand in the south. The nineteenth century found in the land a veritable hodgepodge of nations, ethnic and linguistic groups, and religious belief. Except for the Jews, none regarded Palestine as a homeland, as a national political unity worthy of independence and nationhood. [7]

Mark Twain visited the land in 1867 and wrote in his masterpiece, *The Innocents Abroad*:

Palestine sits in sackcloth and ashes, desolate and unlovely ...

Nazareth is forlorn ... Jericho, the accursed, lies in a moldering ruin. Bethlehem and Bethany, in their poverty and their humiliation, have nothing about them now to remind one that they once knew the high honor of the Savior's presence. [8]

And so it was in the Promised Land. It stands unprecedented in history that a people would, for 2,000 years, pray for and long to return to the homeland from which they were driven so long ago. On every Sabbath, as the Jews are about to open the Synagogue Ark to remove the Torah, they pray:

> *Merciful Father, Deal Kindly with Zion, Rebuild the walls of Jerusalem.*

Heschel passionately demonstrates the view of devout Jews though the ages:

> *The love of this land was due to an imperative, not to an instinct, not to a sentiment. There is a covenant, an engagement of the people to the land. We live by covenants. We could not betray our pledge or discard the promise. When Israel was driven into exile, the pledge became a prayer; the prayer a dream; the dream a passion, a duty, a dedication ... It is a commitment we must not betray. Three thousand years of faithfulness cannot be wiped off. To abandon the land would make a mockery of all our longings, prayer, and commitments. To abandon the land would be to repudiate the Bible.* [9]

David, the great King of Israel, wrote:

> *If I forget you, O Jerusalem, may my right hand forget its skill. May my tongue cling to the roof of my mouth if I do not remember you, if I do not consider Jerusalem my highest joy.*
>
> Psalm 137:5-6

Just as the Jews could never forget Jerusalem, neither could God.

The inerrant voice of prophecy

Consider just a few of the prophecies predicting the return of the Jews to the land:

God says in Isaiah 66:8:

> *Who has ever heard of such a thing? Who has ever seen such things? Can a country be born in a day or a nation be brought forth in a moment? Yet no sooner is Zion in labor than she gives birth to her children.*

Consider the stunning detail of Isaiah 11:11-12:

> *In that day the Lord will reach out his hand a second time to reclaim the remnant that is left of his people*

> *from Assyria, from Lower Egypt, from Upper Egypt, from Cush, from Elam, from Babylonia, from Hamath and from the islands of the sea. He will raise a banner for the nations and gather the exiles of Israel; he will assemble the scattered people of Judah from the four quarters of the earth.*

These words refer to a remarkable worldwide regathering. Isaiah is looking to that day, a reference to the last days. He wrote that God is going to reach out a second time. If this be true, when did God reach out the first time? It occurred in the year 536 B.C. when God regathered the Jewish exiles from Babylon. However, this promise was for a worldwide regathering. This prophecy can only refer to the scattering of the Jewish people in A.D. 70 and their regathering to Israel in 1948. The astonishing statement in verse 12 that God will raise a "banner" for the nations, or set up an ensign or signal as some translations state, is a sign to the nations to release the exiles. It reverberates with the circumstances of our century leading up to the recognition of the Jewish state. No one can hold a twentieth century history of the return of the Jews to Palestine in one hand and Isaiah in the other without a compelling conviction of God's providence.

God's clock is running

When the disciples asked Jesus their three famous questions in Matthew 24:3, they could scarcely separate the three events they pondered:

> *"When will these things be . . . ?"*
>
> = the destruction of the Temple.
>
> *"What will be the sign of your coming . . . ?"*
>
> = the fig tree.

That's right, Jesus said that the generation which sees the fig tree show new signs of life is the generation that would experience His return:

> *Now learn this lesson from the fig tree: As soon as its twigs get tender and its leaves come out, you know that summer is near. Even so, when you see all these things, you know that it is near, right at the door.*
>
> Matthew 24:32-33

God always referred to Israel and the Jewish people in one of two ways. Either as His "vine" or His "fig tree." His fig tree, Israel, was dormant. Why? Because Israel was under the domination of the Romans at the time these words were spoken. In addition, the fig tree would remain dormant and lifeless as the Jewish people would be scattered throughout the world for 1,878 years. We know from our perspective what they could not from theirs. Jesus clearly explained to them the nature of the destruction of the Temple. Against that backdrop, He painted a vivid word picture of His Second Coming and the end of the age. Even though these events were so calamitous that it was difficult for the disciples to separate them, we can see each of them in clear perspective.

Any reading of His comments must take seriously that the return of Israel started a divine clock running. We do not know the exact days, hours, or minutes, but we can know that we are on the last pages of the calendar of world history.

Any discerning Christian can see in the rebirth of Israel and the subsequent events – such as God's providential hand of protection through five Israeli wars – the hand of God in the winding down of history. As I write this, the stage is being set for an irrevocable confrontation between Israeli and Arab. In the surly proclama-tion by Yasser Arafat that he will declare a Palestinian state in the near future and the equally emphatic denial from Israel, the stage for the last great confrontation is being set. As the Oslo Peace Accords unravel, the fuses on both sides are burning short.

The promise of God, over and over again to the Jewish people, is for a return to the land given to them by God Himself. I am convinced May 14, 1948, was the beginning of the final days that will culminate in the coming of Jesus for every true believer in the event we call the Rapture. This will be followed some seven years later by the Second Coming of Christ to the earth. I am further convinced all end-time events depend on Israel being back in the land

God gave to her and that she lost due to her sin and disobedience! It is for this reason the Rebirth of Israel is sign number one. Without the existence of the nation of Israel, we would not be able to say with certainty we are in the last days! I believe this single event, more than any other, is the most prominent sign we are living in the final moments before the coming of Jesus! Therefore, for the true believers in Jesus Christ, we must watch what is happening on a daily basis in Israel, and as we do, we will understand just how little time we have left before the heavens part and Jesus appears to call us home!

6 Dr. G.F. Owens, *Abraham to the Middle East Crisis*, p. 325.

7 Abraham Joshua Heschel, *Israel: An Echo of Eternity*, p. 57.

8 Mark Twain, *The Innocents Abroad* (New York, Harper & Row, 1869)

9 ibid., p. 44.

2
Sign Two: The Reunification of Europe

Just as you saw that the feet and toes
were partly of baked clay and partly of iron,
so this will be a divided kingdom;
yet it will have some of the strength of iron in it,
even as you saw iron mixed with clay.
As the toes were partly iron and partly clay,
so this kingdom will be
partly strong and partly brittle.
Daniel 2:41-42

"Three days ago no one in the world could have predicted this amazing event."

The words we heard on November 12, 1989, were those of then Secretary of State, James Baker. He was speaking of the dismantling of the infamous Berlin Wall, which occurred on November 9. If you watched this event on CNN, as I did, you will recall the people dancing on the wall while the soldiers looked on passively. People were toasting one another with champagne and singing joyously while chipping away huge sections of the wall which had divided Germany for many years. More importantly, it was a symbol of the oppression of the communist government, and now it was coming down.

Little did they know, and few people realized, they were in fact toasting the beginning of a New World Order that will eventually lead to a One World Government prophesied 2,500 years ago!

A dream for all ages

But, was the dismantling of the Berlin Wall in 1989

really the beginning? In order to get the whole story, we must turn back the clock 2,500 years to ancient Babylon. Under the leadership of the powerful new king, Nebuchadnezzar, Babylon had defeated the Egyptians at the Battle of Carchemish in 605 B.C. and had emerged as the new world leader. In that same year, Nebuchadnezzar marched on Jerusalem and carried captive certain articles from the Temple, as well as many of Israel's brightest young minds. Among the captives were Daniel and his three friends, Hananiah, Mishael, and Azariah.

As previously noted, the time of the captivity was to be seventy years, according to God. In the second year of the king's reign, he had a dream that troubled him greatly. He called all his wise men together and told them to tell him his dream and interpret it for him (Daniel 2:1-13). They were shocked! No king had ever requested such a thing from his wise men before, and they said to the king, "Tell us your dream and we will interpret it for you." The king became angry and gave the order for the execution of every wise man in his kingdom. Daniel heard about this, since he was considered to be among the wise men, and he proceeded to do what he always did. He went to God in prayer and God did what He always does. He answered! God gave Daniel the same dream and then He interpreted it for him as well.

In the dream, God showed the king and Daniel a composite history of the remaining days of the world! They saw a great and awesome statue. It had a head of gold, arms and chest of silver, and a stomach and thighs of bronze. Its legs and feet were of iron, with ten toes of part iron and part clay. By the clay we should understand ceramic clay fired in an oven. The toes represented a curious mixture of iron strength and the fragile quality of pottery.

God showed Daniel that the statue was representative of all the kingdoms of the world from his present time until the end of the world. The head of gold symbolized Babylon. The arms and chest of silver represented the Medes and Persians. The stomach and thighs of bronze were symbols of the Greeks.

The Gentiles in Prophecy

Nebuchadnezzar's Dream	**Daniel's Dream**	**The Kingdoms Prophecied**
Gold *(head)*	Lion	Babylonian
Silver (*breast and arms*)	Bear	Medo-Persian
Brass (*belly and thighs*)	Leopard	Greek
Iron (*legs*)	Beast with Iron Teeth	Roman
P R O P H E T I C G A P		
Iron and Clay (*feet*)	Ten Horns	Antichrist
Stone	Son of Man	Jesus Christ

The legs and feet of iron indicated Rome. The ten toes mixed with iron and clay stand for a revived form of the Roman Empire in the final days.

The certainty of God's plans

Now, what does this vision have to do with us in 1998? We have seen the Babylonians fall to the Medes and Persians, just as God said. We have seen the Persians defeated by Alexander the Great and the Greeks, just as God said. We have seen the Greeks fall to the Romans, just as God said. We have seen the collapse of the Romans, just as God said. We are now the generation that has witnessed and is witnessing the coming together of Europe or the revival of the Roman Empire, just as God said!

When the mighty Roman Empire fell, it was not due to an external power, but rather to an internal collapse. Rome, through the worship of her emperors, had introduced into its society every wickedness known to man, and the result was a shredding of the society, which brought about its ultimate decline.

God showed Daniel how Rome would rise again in the final days. Rome, the great ideal of world-wide empire, would return not in exactly the same form as the ancient empire, but rather in a new confederation that would eventually rule the entire world. Hence the vision of a New World Order! In 1990, then President George Bush spoke to the National Religious Broadcasters Convention in Washington, D.C. In his first speech concerning the Gulf War, he outlined his plan for the war with Iraq and then went on to say this:

> *You know what is going to solve all our problems? There is something new called the New World Order! When this comes in, it's going to bring peace like we have never seen. We are going to be able to lay down all of our weapons. The New World Order is the solution to all of our problems!*

When these statements were made, the believers who knew the Scriptures sat up and took note because they recognized the prophetic implication.

The inexorable march to one-world government

I am continuously amazed at how many Christians are passively indifferent to the world events which are taking place and their prophetic significance. The average believer is so entangled in his own day-to-day existence that he is failing to see God's hand in these recent events. In addition, many consider those of us who do to be extremist and somewhat radical.

But was 1989 the real beginning of the New World Order? To better comprehend what is happening, and when the seeds were sown, we need to once again regress historically. The year was 1948. At just about the same time Israel was proclaiming her statehood, a meeting was taking place in Brussels, Belgium, which would lay the foundation for a new organization known as the EEC or European Economic Community. The meeting was called the Benelux Conference and was attended by The Netherlands, Luxembourg and Belgium. These three tiny nations came together because they saw UNITY as their only hope for economic survival in the post-war world! These countries recognized what we all know is true. That is, there is safety and survival in numbers. As the rest of western Europe began to awake from the devastation and reconstruction of the postwar era, they too began to talk in terms of unification. In March of 1957, Italy, France and Germany joined the existing three countries and signed a document known as *The Treaty of Rome*. That document established the Common Market as the administrative headquarters of Europe for trade and transnational dialog. In addition, the treaty set forth guidelines for a network of multinational freedoms consisting of borderless movement of goods, services, capital and people. In 1973, England, Ireland and Denmark aligned themselves and in January 1981, Greece made it a ten-nation confederation. The number grew to twelve on January 1, 1986, as Spain and Portugal cast their lots with the EEC. It was at this same time, 1986, when the EEC officially adopted the goal of a politically unified Europe. The leaders of these countries issued a statement:

> *We realize that it will not be possible for us to move again to world supremacy without unity. Therefore, we must lay aside our differences and come together as a new United States of Europe. By doing this, we will constitute a power bloc that can move to the ascendancy of world leadership.*

On January 1, 1993, the plan went into effect as all trade, tariff and travel restrictions came down among the member nations and a large part of Europe began to function as a united community. The dreams of men like Paul Henri Spaak, a post-World War II premier of Belgium, finally began to come true. Spaak made the following statement during a session of the United Nations General Council in New York:

> *The systems of man have failed. What we need is a leader. What we need is a man. Give us a man to solve*

our problems, and be he a god or a devil, we will follow him.

Jacques Delors, another visionary, authored the famed *Delors Report* that called for uniform economic policies to be imposed upon member nations by the EEC and for the transfer of decision-making power from member countries to the EEC. This report, in effect, meant that the real power would no longer rest in the sovereign nations, but would now lie with a single body and one day, possibly with one man! Think about the ramifications of what we are seeing take shape around us.

The United States of Europe

Today the United States of Europe is the most powerful political force in the world! With a population of over 340 million, it possesses a unified economic strength that is larger than that of America. The United States of Europe is achieving rapid cohesion and cooperation and will on January 1, 1999, merge its currencies into a one-currency system known as the Euro dollar or Eco unit. According to recent news reports, eleven of the twelve member nations will be ready on January 1, 1999, and will put the Euro into exclusive use. Only Greece has delayed due to technical difficulties. This means on January 1, 1999, the United States of Europe will have eleven nations with a combined population of 290 million people functioning economically as one! No longer will we refer to the Germans, British, Dutch, etc., rather these will be known as Europeans!

However, let us not fail to also realize the impact of the new trade policies which have been adopted in the Asian world, Japan and the Pacific Rim, as well as by America, Canada and Mexico. Eventually, in fact, in the very near future, it will become absolutely necessary for the adoption of a single currency worldwide which will ultimately lead to a completely cashless world. Men of vision and understanding have for years seen the inevitable coming. Just think about it. There is the Federal Reserve Bank in

America, the Bank of Japan and the European Central Bank in Europe. These three financial entities could and will one day soon control the wealth of the world. When this day fully arrives, remember the secular substitute for the words of Jesus called the Golden Rule. The secular golden rule is, "he who holds the gold rules." As few as twenty-one people could control the wealth of the world and someone has to be the final authority. The ancient Roman Empire is alive! The future is now! We are the generation living through technological innovations seen by no other society that has ever existed and we have not even discussed debit cards, smart cards, biometrics, microchips and hundreds of other undeniable indicators that we are in the final days, yet all prophesied in the Word of our God as revealed 2,500 years ago to Daniel. It is said familiarity breeds indifference. We dare not be indifferent to the signs of prophetic fulfillment around us. I repeat, the future is now! We must keep our eyes on Israel and the coming together of the rest of the world.

This is in a very real way the assertion of the pride of the Tower of Babel. Humanity wishes to build a great unity against God. The Roman Empire lasted a thousand years, but vanished beneath the combined weight of outside pressure and inside decadence. At the appearance of our Lord Jesus Christ, so also shall this edifice of hubris disappear under the power of His Word.

The mixture of strength and weakness

The mighty statue of ever devolving value in metals tells us another story. Just as Daniel's statue decreased in value as scanned from head to foot, so this weary world has decreased in its commitment to value. Political Darwinians chanted their cant that the world would only get better and better. We now know better. The sublimity of gold resolves into the lesser silver. That disintegrates into bronze. At the end of history the entire, imperious statue stands on a ridiculous mixture of iron and pottery. What a comment this is on the vapid nature of human aspiration without God. What sane man would want a house built on a foundation of pottery and concrete? The end of all human history teeters and totters, like drunks stumbling out of the bar at midnight, on this ridiculous mixture of strength and weakness.

God will bring it to an end. Throughout the cold war the nations trembled that mere mortals would wreck the statue. God did not permit it. That Great Stone cut out without hands long ago seen by Daniel will smash the unbalanced fusion of iron and clay to pieces. Then His Kingdom will fill the earth. Even so, come Lord Jesus. Smash the vile idol of history into a million shards of broken dreams, and make our only dream the reality of Your Kingdom.

3
Sign Three: The Raid of Gog and Magog (The Islamic Invasion)

The word of the LORD came to me:

"Son of man, set your face

against Gog, of the land of Magog ..."

Ezekiel 38:1

I sat somewhat stunned as I watched the scientists move the hands of the infamous Doomsday Clock forward from fourteen minutes until midnight to nine minutes until midnight. I had been listening to news reports of the nuclear testing undertaken by Pakistan. The Pakistanis had stated that one of the reasons they tested their nuclear weapons was to make certain they had the same nuclear prowess as Israel.

"Wait a minute, what does Israel have to do with this?" I asked. The Pakistanis were conducting underground nuclear testing because their neighbor, India, had done so the previous week. How did Israel get into the picture? This is so incredible! This tiny nation of barely six million people is at issue with virtually every nation on earth and especially every Moslem nation in the world. The group of scientists who monitor the world's nuclear weaponry are fearful of the destruction of our world by nuclear weapons. They use words like Armageddon to convey this fear and they maintain a Doomsday Clock, whereby the position of the hands in relation to twelve midnight indicates, in their opinion, how close we are to nuclear "midnight," or destruction. However, the clear teaching of Scripture is that there will be a war which will precede the war of all wars, Armageddon, a war in which God himself will have an active role as He steps in to save the people of Israel from total extinction. While there are many similarities between the war of Ezekiel and the Battle of Armageddon, I believe we are to view these two coming wars as two separate events separated by at least seven years.

This entire scenario is now underscored by the sudden emergence of the mysterious Osama bin Laden. The lightning-like suddenness of his catapult into fame demonstrates how quickly the contemporary world changes. Heir of an enormous fortune, secreted away in Afghanistan, this radical Moslem warrior has declared war on the United States, and of course, Israel. It is not the old war of military machinery, but the insidious new war of terrorism. Yet that malignant war of anonymous cowardice will lead to another armed conflict. This war is described in detail by the prophet Ezekiel in chapters 38 and 39. This is the way Ezekiel described the coming menace in Ezekiel 38:1-8:

> *The word of the LORD came to me: "Son of man, set your face against Gog, of the land of Magog, the chief prince of Meshech and Tubal; prophesy against him and say: 'This is what the Sovereign LORD says: I am against you, O Gog, chief prince of Meshech and Tubal. I will turn you around, put hooks in your jaws and bring you out with your whole army — your horses, your horsemen fully armed, and a great horde with large and small shields, all of them brandishing their swords. Persia, Cush and Put will be with them, all with shields and helmets, also Gomer with all its troops, and Beth Togarmah from the far north with all its troops — the many nations with you. Get ready; be prepared, you and all the hordes gathered about you, and take command of them. After many days you will be called to arms. In future years you will invade a land that has recovered from*

war, whose people were gathered from many nations to the mountains of Israel, which had long been desolate. They had been brought out from the nations, and now all of them live in safety.'"

Who is Gog and Magog?

This great battle has been called the War of Gog and Magog; however, a more accurate title might be the "Islamic Invasion." This is a war in which the Moslem nations of the world will finally unite against Israel and with determination set out to destroy her once and for all. God has a different idea, however. I will not attempt to describe each and every nation mentioned in this prophetic passage, but will say Russia is a major player. I think it is interesting to note that the Great Wall of China was built to keep Russia from invading China, and in Arabic it is called Al Magog.

The former Soviet Union and the Russia of today have always been anti-Israel and pro-Moslem. It was the former Soviet Union which in April 1967, aggravated the situation with Syria and Egypt, which ultimately led to the Six Day War in June of that same year. The Soviet Union was an agitator as well in the Yom Kippur War of 1973. In addition, the Soviets were responsible for the large supply of Russian-made weaponry discovered in May of 1982 in southern Lebanon. This weaponry apparently was to be used for a massive invasion of Israel from Lebanon. Upon the discovery of such a massive amount of equipment, the Israeli Defense Forces invaded southern Lebanon and established a forty-mile security zone. In fact, there was so much Russian military equipment discovered that the Israelis started a cottage industry selling used, confiscated Russian equipment to other countries and they profited quite nicely.

The crisis in the former Soviet Union

It is important as one recognizes the present situation in Russia and observes the financial crisis in its midst to understand that Russia's finances have all but disintegrated. She is desperate for an infusion of foreign currency, especially dollars, if she is to survive, and the begging bowl is out once again. How and where can this life-saving infusion come from?

First, the International Monetary Fund has already loaned Russia millions since 1989. Now Russia is asking for ten to fifteen billion dollars more in financial aid from the IMF. According to the Associated Press releases on July 10, 1998, President Yeltsin has promised to put Russia's fiscal house in order if he can get this loan. He has called on a series of Western leaders, including President Clinton, beseeching them for aid in this crisis, and he will not be denied by the fearful West. In addition to IMF loans, Russia has agreed to sell nuclear arms to Iran and the two nations have joined together to work on nuclear projects. Russia has further agreed to sell two nuclear power stations to India. These facts were revealed via the well known and highly respected *Jane's Defense Weekly* released July 5, 1998. As Russia pleads for help financially, she is aiding the anti-Israel world to prepare themselves for nuclear war. Make no mistake about it, the Big Bear may be injured but she isn't out of the game. Russia will be the major player in this battle on the mountains of Israel.

This instability has been underscored in the firing of the Russian cabinet for the second time in a few months by beleaguered Boris Yeltsin. The basis for the dismissal was the economic instability of the Russian economy.

The fearsome alliance to come

In addition to Russia, it is sufficient to say that the Moslem nations, which made up a large part of the former Soviet Union until November 1989, will be willing participants. Countries such as Kazakhstan, Uzbekistan, Kyrgyzstan and others will forge an alliance against Israel. In addition, Ethiopia, the Sudan, Lebanon, Syria, Jordan, Iran, Iraq, Saudia Arabia, the Gulf Emirates, Yemen, Egypt, Algeria and every other Moslem nation will finally unite against tiny Israel. Their goal will be the total annihilation of

Israel. God, however, will intervene and destroy these nations upon the mountains of Israel.

When could such an event like this take place? There are numerous scholars who agree that this invasion will take place just prior to the Rapture of the Church or simultaneous with it. I agree with this position and, as I follow daily events in the Middle East, I believe we are on the very threshold of this frightening event. This devastating denouement will bring massive death and destruction to millions of unsuspecting souls.

What are the possible scenarios that could bring about such an invasion of Israel by Russia and the Islamic world?

Scenario number one: The attempted destruction of the Dome of the Rock

Each time I walk up the earthen ramp leading to Temple Mount in Jerusalem, I think of General Moshe Dayan of the Israeli Defense Forces. It was June 1967, and Israel had defeated Egypt, Jordan and

Syria. The city of Jerusalem, divided since 1948, was now about to be united once again. For the first time since A.D. 70, the Jewish people would be allowed to pray at their Wailing Wall, also known as the Western Wall. The people of Israel were exuberant. In the hours following their great victory, General Dayan made a decision which has haunted the people of Israel ever since. General Dayan decided to allow the defeated Moslems to continue to exercise control over the thirty-five acres known as Temple Mount. The Moslem shrine, the Dome of the Rock, was there, as well as the Al Aksa Mosque. It was an attempt at reconciliation. It failed! Chaim Herzog, President of Israel in the years 1983-1994, writes in his memoirs:

> *We reached the Lion's Gate overcome by emotion. I had been to the Old City with my father during the British Mandate, but now it was ours. The dream had come true. For 2,000 years, every day, three times a day, observant Jews had prayed, "May our eyes see Your return to Zion." The longing for the Old City and*

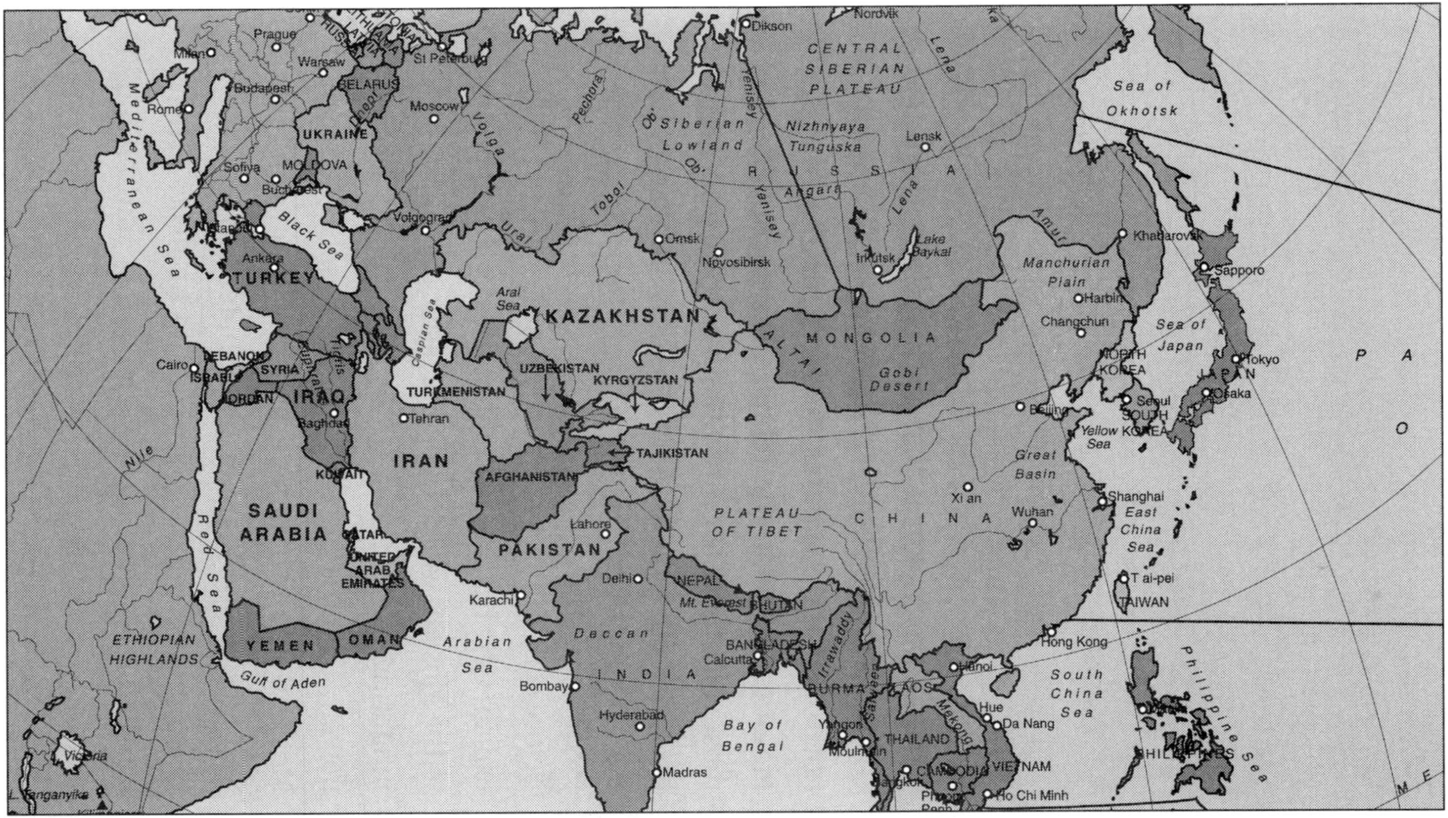

Islamic Nations Surrounding Israel

> *the Wailing Wall was palpable. An Israeli flag had been hoisted in celebration – and Dayan's first order was to haul it down. He did not want to offend Moslem sensibilities.* [10]

General Dayan knew that if the Israelis had any chance of peace with the Islamic world, they could not touch the Dome of the Rock or the Al Aksa Mosque. This spot, the Temple Mount, could be the most volatile piece of real estate in the world, and a hotbed of emotion for both Moslems and Jews.

A brief history

Before continuing, I feel it would be helpful to briefly explain why the Temple Mount area is so important to the Moslem world. Upon the death of Mohammed, infighting began between two rival caliphs seeking power. Eventually, this led to a split between Moslems into two major groups, the Shiites and the Sunnites, called Sunnies. The Shiites sought a way to keep the Sunnies from coming to Mecca. Their problem was solved, so they thought, by starting and spreading a lie that became accepted as fact. The lie was that Mohammed had flown from Mecca to Jerusalem on his winged horse named El Baruk. As the story goes, he landed on what is Temple Mount at the site of the great rock where Abraham was prepared to sacrifice his son (Ishmael according to Moslems; Isaac according to the Bible). Mohammed later departed into heaven from this same spot. Therefore this made the location holy to the Moslems and they constructed the Dome of the Rock on this site in the years A.D. 687-91 and encouraged the Sunnies to worship there instead of Mecca. *The Koran*, the Moslem holy book, does not help with this confusion since it was not even composed until A.D. 933, three centuries after Mohammed's death.

A bomb waiting to explode

Since the Temple Mount is sacred to the Moslem world, one can imagine what the reaction would be if something were to happen to it. Ever since 1967 there have been those who have sought to destroy the Dome of the Rock, the Al Aksa mosque, purify the ground with the ashes of a red heifer and rebuild the Temple on its original site. I will deal with this movement in greater detail in the chapter on the "Rebuilding of the Temple."

However, it is important to note that if something were to happen to the sacred Moslem sites, this one event could rally the entire Moslem world to come against Israel. But why would Russia lead the way? Perhaps it could be that Russia, in woeful financial straits, sees this as an opportunity to gain control of the assets of the Moslem world by standing with them in this struggle, especially since Russia is the one who supplies their weapons. The Moslem world would most certainly be concerned regarding America's response to such an invasion, and Russia could convince them that its presence would neutralize America. This is only one of the possible scenarios. Do keep in mind, however, we have an explosive equation, the hatred of the Jews by the Moslems coupled with the need for survival by the Russians. Could it be?

Scenario number two: Israel says "No" to Syria

The second possible scenario, which could light the fuse of the Middle East and bring the Islamic world upon Israel, relates to Syria and its president, Hafez Assad. In the Six Day War of 1967, Israel pushed the Syrians out of the Golan Heights and dealt Assad an embarrassing blow to his "honor." Since that time, Syria has often demanded the return of the Golan Heights. Following the Yom Kippur War of October 1973, when Israel once again defeated Syria and Egypt, the United Nations placed a peacekeeping presence in the Heights and they remain to the present. Israel annexed the Golan Heights and made them a part of Israel on December 14, 1981, which further aggravated Assad. A vital point in the peace negotiations has been whether or not Israel will return the Golan to Syrian control. Israel has repeatedly maintained it would be impossible to provide for the safety and security of the Jewish population living in upper Galilee without the

Golan. Therefore the answer to date has been a clear and consistent "No." However, having stated this, we need to look at the events which led to the assassination of former Prime Minister Rabin.

A private meeting

I personally had the privilege of meeting with Prime Minister Rabin at his office in Jerusalem in July 1995. This meeting had been arranged by a friend of Dr. W.A. Criswell, pastor emeritus of First Baptist Church, Dallas, Texas. In addition to Dr. Criswell and me, Dr. O.S. Hawkins, then pastor of First Baptist Church, Ft. Lauderdale, Florida was present. The three of us spent approximately forty-five minutes with the prime minister and the meeting was enlightening to say the least. Mr. Rabin was frank, friendly and very warm to the three of us. Near the end of this meeting, I asked the prime minister if he would consider agreeing to three things:

1 Consider giving up the Golan Heights to Syria;

2 Allow a Palestinian State on Israeli soil;

3 Permit Jerusalem to become the capital of a Palestinian state.

He answered that he would not permit any of these three things to come to pass. He particularly said he would not give up the Golan and that he did not see this as a viable option to peace with the Syrians. I stated to him that the reason I posed these questions was because I felt if he were to come out in favor of any of these three things, he could possibly be the first Jewish leader to be assassinated by his own people. The reason I stated this was because of the depth of the emotions of Israeli families. Almost every family in Israel lost brothers, sons and fathers on those hills during the two previous wars. Over 4,000 Jewish lives were lost in 1973 alone. To allow Syria to take control over the Golan again would be saying in a sense, "The lives of your fathers, sons and brothers meant nothing." Mr. Rabin smiled at me and said, "That will never happen; Jews don't kill Jews."

Shortly after my meeting with the prime minister it was learned that Foreign Minister Peres

ANOTHER TRADOR.

and the prime minister had in principle agreed to return the Golan. Apparently by way of a private letter delivered to Assad, they informed him that he could have the Golan Heights; there were just a few details yet to be worked out. Apparently, one of the details involved a United Nations' peacekeeping force that would remain in the Golan to assure Israel of peace. I was amazed in the ensuing weeks to read of the concerted efforts of Prime Minister Rabin and Foreign Minister Peres as they sought to sell the Jewish people on this idea. I remember vividly as my wife Sandra and I drove through the Golan near Caesarea Philippi seeing the thousands of marchers protesting this very idea by burning tires and encouraging signatures on petitions.

I was amazed that Prime Minister Rabin tried to calm the concerns of the Israelis by promoting the idea that the Golan would only be occupied by the Syrians, provided a U.N. peacekeeping force would be deployed. Apparently, the record of the failures of the United Nations and their ability to keep peace was either overlooked or ignored.

A striking letter

In the December 31, 1994, edition of the *Jerusalem Post International,* a most interesting letter was written to Prime Minister Rabin from a Jewish doctor now living in Michigan. The letter was so insightful I filed away a copy. Dr. J.S. Kaufman wrote and reminded Prime Minister Rabin that prior to the Six Day War in June of 1967, then dictator of Egypt, General Gamal Abdel Nasser, ordered the U.N. Emergency Force stationed in the Sinai to withdraw from their observation posts along the Israeli-Egyptian border. The matter was never brought before the United Nations General Assembly, rather Secretary-General U. Thant complied and ordered the forces to vacate within forty-eight hours, abandoning Israel. Dr. Kaufman further stated:

> *What might be of interest to Mr. Rabin is the action of the Serbs (in the Bosnia-Herzegovina-Sarajevo war) vis-a-vis the great power of NATO and the U.N.*

They have treated them with utter contempt. Despite all the dire warnings coming from these august and all-powerful bodies, the Serbs have persisted in their lethal objectives. They have, within the last few days, added insult to injury and actually taken over 400 U.N. peace-keepers as political hostages. Of course, the U.S. role in these proceedings has been even less distinguished.

Are these the world forces that Mr. Rabin is expecting to protect Israel from Syria, Palestinian Arabs, Iraq, Iran and Saudia Arabia once Mr. Rabin has given up Israel's vital defensive positions on the Golan Heights and in the mountains of Judea and Samaria?

Having understood the absolute necessity of keeping the Golan Heights under Israeli control and the emotions attached to this place, one can better understand, while certainly not agree with or approve of, the events which led to Mr. Rabin's assassination in November 1995. This led to the ascendency to the prime minister's office by Shimon Peres and finally to the defeat of the Labor Party in the ensuing elections of May 1996. The Israelis elected a young conservative, Binyamin Netanyahu, as prime minister by voting in the Likud Party. The Likud Party was elected for two reasons: they promised to stop the wholesale giveaway of Israeli land, and they vowed not to give up the Golan Heights. Understanding this, we can now clearly see the scenario for a possible war with Syria that could ignite the short fuse, and end up encouraging Russia and the entire Moslem world.

Assad's reaction

What happens in Syria when Prime Minister Netanyahu finally announces a steadfast "NO" to the request of Syria for the return of the Golan to their control? Remember, honor, saving face, is the most important issue to a Moslem, and Assad wants the Golan to save face with the Syrian people.

Since the Gulf War, Syria has spent millions

upon millions of dollars to acquire the most sophisticated missile arsenal in the Middle East. During the writing of this book, the *Jerusalem Post International* edition reported July 4, 1998:

> *Syria will soon be capable of producing C-Scud missles and VX-type nerve gas, a senior military intelligence officer reportedly told the Knesset Foreign Affairs and Defense Committee last week. Defense Minister Yitzhak Mordechai told the committee that Syria is continuing to hold military exercises and to equip itself with anti-tank weapons, which can also be used to attack. Earlier in the week, President Ezer Weizman warned that Syria remains the chief military threat to the country. "The Syrian threat is much closer than that of Iran or Iraq," Weizman said. "It (Syria) has many missiles and they have high accuracy."*

Jane's Defense Weekly, an intelligence report, echoed these same concerns during the week of July 11, 1998:

> *"Syria is now set to produce the deadly VX nerve*

> *agent." The report stated, "Syria is already able to produce other chemical agents." Who are they going to use these biological and chemical weapons on?*

I believe it is entirely possible when Assad realizes once and for all that neither the United States, the United Nations, the European Economic Community nor world opinion can pressure the Israelis into giving up the Golan, he may finally act. It is possible he will fire chemical carrying Scud missles on Haifa and Tel Aviv. He would not launch missles at Jerusalem because of the Moslem holy sites. It is also probable that when he does this, Israel will retaliate with a nuclear strike on Damascus. Seven hundred forty years before Jesus, the prophet Isaiah wrote these words recorded in Isaiah 17:1:

> *See, Damascus will no longer be a city but will become a heap of ruins.*

Damascus will be left in ruins

One of the ways a student of prophecy determines

whether a prophecy has already been fulfilled or is yet to be fulfilled is to look at history. As one looks at history one might ask, "Has this ever happened before in the history of the world?" When one researches this prophecy, one finds that according to historical sources the city of Damascus is the oldest continuously inhabited city in the world. Therefore we can say with certainty this prophecy is futuristic and is yet to be fulfilled.

Syria fires on Israel. Israel retaliates, and this action both angers Russia and rallies the Moslem world. America doesn't have the resolve to defend Israel any longer because our own internal problems are too great, and Americans are increasingly growing weary of being the world's police force. In addition, we have lost the respect of the world. This could be the catalyst that finally brings the Moslem world together. Their numbers have always dwarfed the Jews, but they have never been able to rally together and put aside their individual differences to destroy Israel. It seems each of the Moslem dictators wants to be the big dog to lead the pack. We all know that there is room for only one head coach on any team. God himself described the descendants of Ishmael, the Arabs, when He said:

> *He will be a wild donkey of a man; his hand will be against everyone and everyone's hand against him, and he will live in hostility toward all his brothers."*
>
> Genesis 16:12

We have witnessed this ourselves with Mu'Ammar Qadhafi, Hafez Assad, Yasser Arafat, Saddam Hussein and other Moslem leaders. This action by Assad then leads the Moslem world and Russia to attack. God intervenes and destroys them supernaturally on the mountains of Israel.

Scenario number three: Iraq

I awoke on the morning of August 2, 1990, poured my coffee and turned on CNN. I was shocked, yet not surprised, to hear the reports that Iraq had invaded its brother Kuwait. For months Saddam Hussein had been insisting that Kuwait and the United Arab

Emirates had been flooding the international market with oil, causing a reduction in price with heavy financial losses to Iraq. In fact, he accused the Kuwaitis of stealing two million dollars in oil sales from him. Most of the western world had been ignoring Saddam's threats, viewing the problem as a regional squabble. It was assumed that once the oil prices were compromised, the inter-Arab struggle would disappear. In addition, Saddam was claiming the land of Kuwait rightly belonged to his kingdom. He maintained that it had been separated illegally by the British, who granted Kuwait independence in 1961, and he wanted it back. However, at the root of the issue once again was the insatiable desire of the Moslem to dominate. Saddam was testing the waters once again. If he could take Kuwait and the world merely stand by, then he could likewise move against the Arab Emirates, Saudi Arabia and who knows where next.

It is the untamed thirst for power! On August 2, he made his move. Sixty divisions of the Iraqi military moved against tiny Kuwait and took control of the entire country in a matter of hours. His action was condemned not only by the free world but by the Arab world as well. Notable exceptions were King Hussein of Jordan, the Yemenites, and the PLO. Once again the world was watching Arab Moslem against Arab Moslem, just as it had in the seven-year war between Iran and Iraq.

Modern-day Nebuchadnezzar

What did Israel have to do with this crisis? As the days passed, Saddam began to feel as though he was going to pull off this invasion. The more confident he grew, the louder he began to boast. He began to threaten Israel. He made statements in which he threatened to "burn half of Israel" by firing missles with chemical warheads. He began to see himself as the modern-day Nebuchadnezzar, ruler of ancient Babylon, who would attack and defeat the Jews. In the meantime, the Israelis were being told by the United States, the European Community and Russia to exercise restraint. President Bush was pressuring then Prime Minister Yitzhak Shamir because the consensus was that, if Israel answered Saddam's threats, it would divert world focus from the Kuwait invasion. The United Nations had set a deadline of January 15, 1991, for Iraq's withdrawal from Kuwait. As the deadline approached, it became apparent to everyone that there would be no withdrawal. Saddam was not about to give in to world pressure. Once again the world exhibited its lack of understanding of the Moslem mentality.

The first televised war

For the first time in the history of the world, we witnessed via satellite a war on the other side of the globe. On January 16, the attack began and for the next 100 days, this was the major topic of world conversation. On this same day, Saddam Hussein fired Scud missles on Israel for the first time. Rockets landed in Ramat Gan and Azur near Tel Aviv. The very next night a large area in Ramat Gan was destroyed. Several weeks later I personally inspected this area and was amazed that so little loss of life had occurred. Scud missles continued to fall in the Tel Aviv area for the next several nights, to the shouts of joy from the Palestinians and Yasser Arafat, who had sided with Saddam. History, of course, records the outcome of the Gulf War: in 100 days the coalition forces defeated Saddam. However, what has not been written is what the final outcome will be. Saddam Hussein will not comply with United Nations' sanctions and the U.N. will eventually either go back to war with Iraq, compromise and weaken the sanctions against him (this is already taking place), or simply lose the resolve to stand against him.

Suppose, however, he continues to defy the U.N. and the United States leads the way in further military action (this time we would probably be alone with the exception of England). Saddam has already made it clear that if another invasion comes from the West, he will unleash his arsenal of nerve gas on Israel. I can assure you if he moves to do this, Israel will not stand idly by this time, but will fire on Baghdad. This could ignite the Russians and the rest of the Jew-hating Moslem world.

Any one or more of the above possible scenarios could take place, or perhaps other events which have yet to transpire, could bring God's Word to fulfillment. The stage is set. The players are in place. It could happen at any moment. Keep your eye on the Middle East!

How strange it is that those desert lands, peopled by the ancient empires so long vanished, continue to be the center of world attention. While history's focus moved to the West, those lands bided their time. Now in the twilight of civilization, they emerge exactly on time in the biblical timetable. The wheels of Providence grind slowly, but they grind exceedingly fine. Man's power is noisy. God's powerful purpose in history flows like a river through the night, inexorably cutting its course through time to the fulfillment of God's purposes.

[10] Chaim Herzog, *Living History*, p. 171.

4
Sign Four: The Revealing of the Antichrist

There before me was another horn
... This horn had eyes
like the eyes of a man and a mouth
that spoke boastfully.
Daniel 7:8

Paul Henry Spaak, the former premier of Belgium and a proponent of a one-world government, made this striking statement in the General Session of the United Nations several years ago:

> *The systems of man have failed, what we need is a leader, what we need is a man! Be he a god or be he the devil, let him come and we will follow him!*

Mr. Spaak was expressing the frustration of the nations of the world in trying to solve the mounting problems which plague our world. His statement expressed his belief that the answer lies in a leader, a man who can bring the peoples and nations of the world together in unity and peace. You see, even though Europe is coming together, someone has to be at the helm! Will there be such a man? The Bible prophesies exactly that in the final days. He is called "the prince who will come!"

Humanity's endless desire for a world leader

The pages of history are replete with humanity's cry

for a man, any man, who is the consummate warrior and leader of humankind. The ancient Assyrians craved such a leader in Ashurbanipal and Tiglath Pileser. The Babylonians produced a Nobonidus and a Nebuchadnezzar. The latter incarnated such overweening pride that he had his name stamped on every brick of every building of Babylon: "Great is Nebuchadnezzar son of Nabopolassar." The walls of his palace could support the racing of two chariots side-by-side. Yet he fell under the shadow of the magnificent Cyrus, the instrument of Jehovah, though Cyrus knew it not. Cyrus himself was overshadowed by Alexander the Great. The mighty Macedonian pushed his Greek army for ten years, all the way to the Indus River. He died in ancient Babylon of a fever following a bout of drinking. His empire was divided among his generals, the Seleucids and the Ptolomies. Humanity craves a great warrior, who will, in Alexander's words, cause all humankind to drink as from a loving cup.

On the ashen remnants of the Greek Empire was

built the mighty iron empire of Rome. To flee her was impossible, and to resist her was death. The pompous Pompey or the vain Julius Caesar were the renewed embodiments of humanity's desire for a regal leader who knows all and wins all. That mantle fell on Augustus and those who followed him into the twilight of the Roman Empire. That same impulse led to the rise of Charlemagne, a man so powerful he welded together the Frankish peoples, but so ignorant he could not read his own signature. The cry of the peoples of all times is, "Give us a man, and we will follow."

The people demand a leader who is the embodiment of power and authority. Whether a Peter the Great of Russia or a Charles V of the Holy Roman Empire, they endlessly crave the same thing. Give us a leader who will weld humanity together as one.

You may go to the massively domed Invalides in Paris. Under the striking spectacle of a mighty dome you enter into the burial place of Napoleon. The Corsican Empire builder is buried in a massive porphyry casket of rusted red hue. Around that casket are statues and inscriptions that recapitulate his victories in the building of the French empire. Today people parade into that tomb from all over the planet seeking to see the resting place of the world empire builder. Their presence at Invalides is a mute testimony to unending desire for a man, any man, who holds all power.

At the end of the twentieth century people still have an interest in Adolph Hitler that cannot be slacked. Why does humanity continue to lust after knowledge for this greatest demon of the twentieth century? We desire to know of him for the same reason the German people were hypnotized and mesmerized at the Nuremberg rallies. Hitler personifies our unabated desire to have a man, any man, who will, with power and godlike authority, bring an answer to the quandaries of humanity that have no evident solution.

What shall we make of this long line of emperors and potentates, pharaohs and caesars, czars and kings, rulers and demagogues? They are, all of them, a foreshadowing of that one last satanic masterpiece, the antichrist.

Jesus warned of the coming of antichrist

In the last precious hours that Jesus spent with the Twelve, He reserved time to discuss the end. As part of that discussion, He solemnly warned them of those who would come and take upon themselves His place:

> *At that time if anyone says to you, "Look, here is the Christ!" or, "There he is!" do not believe it. For false Christs and false prophets will appear and perform great signs and miracles to deceive even the elect — if that were possible. See, I have told you ahead of time. So if anyone tells you, "There he is, out in the desert," do not go out; or, "Here he is, in the inner rooms," do not believe it.*
>
> Matthew 24:23-26

At the threshold of His own Passion, our Lord surveys the unfolding ages to come. He presents an ever-escalating frenzy that will produce the final satanic masterpiece. He warns His people in every age, and particularly at the final age, to beware of the pseudo-Christ and pseudo-prophets. What is the pseudo-Christ? In any generation and era, any epoch and century, it is that person who arrogates to himself the position and power that belong to Christ alone. There have been such in each of twenty centuries of the Christian era. They are, all of them, precursors and foreshadowings, harbingers and augurs, of that final, unspeakable incarnation of human evil, the antichrist of biblical warning.

Our Lord's words concerning these manifestations are as chilling and sobering as they are warning and helpful. These midget messiahs, these Jesus-wannabes, will by demonic power demonstrate striking signs and works of power that will leave people astonished. They are all foreshadowing that final great antichrist who will dazzle humanity with works of undeniable power. Our Lord's admonition is clear: do not follow them. If a great horde of people march into the desolation of the desert to see a numinous miracle worker, do not go. If some maddened crowd seeks to pry open the door of a secret chamber where the Christ is supposed to be seated in splendid power, leave them to their own devices. Let them follow Geraldo in such lunacy of speculation and invasion of secret places. None of that belongs to our Lord Jesus Christ. For His own people, He is the Lord of the trumpet blast and the archangel's cry. Look not for Him in some salacious article in the *National Enquirer*. Look for Him in the breaking dawn of His rapturous return for His Church. Seek Him in His Second Coming at the defeat of the antichrist, when He will reign with power and authority from Jerusalem.

The beloved disciple likewise warned of the antichrist

The last surviving eyewitness among the Twelve was

the beloved disciple John. He lived until the end of the first Christian century. As part of his warning to the believers of the era he wrote:

> *Dear children, this is the last hour; and as you have heard that the antichrist is coming, even now many antichrists have come. This is how we know it is the last hour.*
>
> 1 John 2:18

In this remarkable warning, the apostle makes several assertions important for our study. He could write at the end of the first Christian century that it was "the last time." That is to say, there has been nothing that could prevent the imminent return of the Lord Jesus Christ at the Rapture to snatch away His people before the Tribulation. Further, John makes it clear that the teaching concerning the antichrist was part of the most elementary Christian instruction. He can assume that his readers knew of the fact and the coming of the antichrist. He did not have to introduce them to that fact as if it were some unusual or esoteric doctrine. The teaching concerning the antichrist is rooted in the earliest instruction of Christians.

This should not be a surprise, for the Jews themselves had long taught the expectation of an antimessiah, whose name in Jewish lore was Armilus. The Jews themselves assumed that when the messiah appeared, there would follow at some time an antimessiah.

Of course, the statement of John intrigues us with the assertion that by the end of the first Christian century there were already "many antichrists." We are to understand thereby that the great, final antichrist will be preceded by many lesser antichrists whose spirit he will incarnate in one final manifestation of absolute evil. For example, the early Christians considered Nero to be an antichrist. The church father Commodianus of North Africa identified him as such. Nero was the first worldy manifestation of that satanic spirit that will ultimately manifest itself in the antichrist, a personage who I believe is alive today.

The vision of Daniel and the antichrist

Once again we turn to Daniel, only this time to the seventh chapter and this time it has to do with four beasts which rise up from the earth!

> *In the first year of Belshazzar king of Babylon, Daniel had a dream, and visions passed through his mind as he was lying on his bed. He wrote down the substance of his dream. Daniel said: "In my vision at night I looked, and there before me were the four winds of heaven churning up the great sea. Four great beasts, each different from the others, came up out of the sea. The first was like a lion, and it had the wings of an eagle. I watched until its wings were torn off and it was lifted from the ground so that it stood on two feet like a man, and the heart of a man was given to it. And there before me was a second beast, which looked like a bear. It was raised up on one of its sides, and it had three ribs in its mouth between its teeth. It was told, 'Get up and eat your fill of flesh!' After that, I looked, and there before me was another beast, one that looked like a leopard. And on its*

back it had four wings like those of a bird. This beast had four heads, and it was given authority to rule. After that, in my vision at night I looked, and there before me was a fourth beast—terrifying and frightening and very powerful. It had large iron teeth; it crushed and devoured its victims and trampled underfoot whatever was left. It was different from all the former beasts, and it had ten horns. While I was thinking about the horns, there before me was another horn, a little one, which came up among them; and three of the first horns were uprooted before it. This horn had eyes like the eyes of a man and a mouth that spoke boastfully."

Daniel 7:1-8

Daniel sees that from the revived form of the Roman Empire, the European Union, a little horn rises who is none other than the false messiah, the antichrist. I call him Satan's Superman because he really will be able to stop speeding locomotives and leap over tall buildings in a single bound! The Bible says this man will rule over the world for a period of seven years, which it calls the "time of Jacob's trouble" (Jeremiah 30:7), but we know it better as the Trial and Tribulation Period recorded in Revelation 6-19:11.

In his dramatic dream, Daniel saw this mighty manifestation of evil arising out of the sea. For the biblical Jew, the sea was that untamed chaos that would swallow up the dry land if God did not contain it. For a creature to come out of the stormy sea was the apocalyptic vision of a creature arising out of humanity's chaos. The horn is a symbol in biblical language of ravaging strength. Even today, the horn of the rodeo bull provides the thrill as we watch a bull rider. It is the pointed, hard, stabbing and flesh-tearing possibility that belongs to the horn. The "little horn" is filled with eyes. This is a gruesome combination of savage, brute strength and intelligence. In the coded language of apocalyptic visions, this "little horn" combines the terror of strength with the knowledge of intelligence. What a dramatic way to describe the final antichrist.

Not only does Scripture say he will rule the world, but that he will be a miracle worker and the whole world will willingly, of their own volition, follow after him!

To the Jews, he will be the Messiah; to the Moslems, the long-awaited Immam or Maitreya; to those who are calling themselves Christian, since the true believers will have already exited this world in the Rapture of the Church, he will be the Christ! In reality, he is satan incarnate!

By the way, some in the charismatic movement of today, as well as those who teach dominion theology, are unintentionally and unknowingly getting their followers ready to receive the antichrist. Why is this true? Because they declare miracles to be the proof of God's blessing and power. The antichrist and the false prophet are going to be the greatest miracle workers the world has seen since Jesus. In addition, they are teaching their followers that by electing Christians to political offices and through overcoming evil in our world, we are going to usher in a golden era of peace. The Church is going to dominate the world. It is an idea that sounds great, but it simply isn't going to happen according to Scripture. It is actually a new revision of the formerly popular post-millennial viewpoint. That viewpoint is rooted in the nineteenth century's optimism that scientific and political progress would build the Kingdom of God, and that conditions on earth would get better and better. The cruelty of two world wars, the depression and the atomic age demonstrated that misplaced optimism is forever wrong. The only change in our weary world will be the direct intervention of God in the return of Jesus Christ. No political program can abate the flood of unbelief and cruelty in the godless world.

A matter of definition

We hear the term antichrist and perhaps fail to grasp its full meaning. The Greek prefix *anti* can mean "opposed to" or "against," but it can also mean "in the place of" or "a substitute for." What am I saying? Simply this: the antichrist will be both opposed to God and a substitute for God! He will pretend to be Jesus!

Let me give you a quick review of what the Scriptures say about this man:

1. He will come with a program for peace (Daniel 8:25).
2. He will persecute and kill those who get saved during the tribulation (Daniel 7:25).
3. He will come from the area of the ancient Roman Empire (Daniel 9:26).
4. He will make a seven-year peace treaty with Israel that will allow her to rebuild her temple (Daniel 9:27).
5. He will break the treaty with Israel after three and one-half years (Daniel 9:27).
6. He will occupy the rebuilt temple in Jerusalem (2 Thessalonians 2:4).
7. He will suffer what appears to be a mortal wound and will seemingly be resurrected like Jesus (Revelation 13:14-15).

Somewhere at this moment there may be a young man growing to maturity. He is in all likelihood a brooding, thoughtful young man. Inside his heart, however, there is a hellish rage. It boils like a caldron of molten lead. He hates God. He despises Jesus Christ. He detests the Church. In his mind there is taking shape the form of a dream of conquest. He will disingenuously present himself as a friend of Christ and the Church. Yet beneath this veneer of civility, there is a Trojan horse. He will, once empowered, pour out hell itself onto this world. Can the world produce such a prodigy? Hitler was once a little boy. Stalin was a lad. Nero was a child. The tenderness of childhood will be shaped by the devil into the terror of the antichrist.

The amoral, callous and depraved world of our day is ripe for the deception of just such a leader. Is he alive today? I believe he is, and that he is standing by in the wings awaiting his moment to step onto the world stage! But how could it happen?

5
Sign Five: The Rise of a One-World Religion

Then I saw another beast,

coming out of the earth.

He had two horns like a lamb,

but he spoke like a dragon.

Revelation 13:11

Then I saw another beast, coming out of the earth. He had two horns like a lamb, but he spoke like a dragon. He exercised all the authority of the first beast on his behalf, and made the earth and its inhabitants worship the first beast, whose fatal wound had been healed. And he performed great and miraculous signs, even causing fire to come down from heaven to earth in full view of men. Because of the signs he was given power to do on behalf of the first beast, he deceived the inhabitants of the earth. He ordered them to set up an image in honor of the beast who was wounded by the sword and yet lived. He was given power to give breath to the image of the first beast, so that it could speak and cause all who refused to worship the image to be killed. He also forced everyone, small and great, rich and poor, free and slave, to receive a mark on his right hand or on his forehead, so that no one could buy or sell unless he had the mark, which is the name of the beast or the number of his name.

Revelation 13:11-17

One of the seven angels who had the seven bowls came and said to me, "Come, I will show you the punishment of the great prostitute, who sits on many waters. With her the kings of the earth committed adultery and the inhabitants of the earth were intoxicated with the wine of her adulteries." Then the angel carried me away in the Spirit into a desert. There I saw a woman sitting on a scarlet beast that was covered with blasphemous names and had seven heads and ten horns. The woman was dressed in purple and scarlet, and was glittering with gold, precious stones and pearls. She held a golden cup in her hand, filled with abominable things and the filth of her adulteries. This title was written on her forehead:

MYSTERY

BABYLON THE GREAT

THE MOTHER OF PROSTITUTES

AND OF THE ABOMINATIONS OF THE EARTH.

I saw that the woman was drunk with the blood of the saints, the blood of those who bore testimony to Jesus. When I saw her, I was greatly astonished.

Revelation 17:1-6

In the second sign, the reunification of Europe, we have seen that commercial, political and military unity is being achieved by the United States of Europe. However, there is an even greater bond needed to strengthen the ties that bind these nations and mold them into a single entity. That bond is religious unity! A call is coming forth for the unity of all faiths (a common one-world faith for everyone). The world is crying, in fact demanding, PEACE, PEACE! In order for there to be peace, the religions of the world must unify. That clarion call is coming from the Vatican, headquarters of the Roman Catholic Church. In the past thirty-five years, since the close of the Second Vatican Council, the Catholic Church has been building bridges into all of the world's religions. There was agreement in 1965 that the strategy of control and domination by fear had to change. Their goal then became to unite all people under the authority of the Roman pontiff by outward acceptance of other beliefs, but without inward change. In other words, Vatican II repackaged Catholicism. I am always amazed at how newly updated, current packaging can sell an old product which has not changed internally. Consider what Pope John Paul II had to say as he addressed the need for European unity on the feast of the Ascension in 1998.

> *Italy is called to contribute in its own way so that, in the new Europe, the Christian faith might be life-giving leaven and cement which unifies.* [11]

The Roman Catholic Church has become one of the most powerful authorities in global affairs and its influence is felt in virtually every nation on earth. How does Rome wield so much influence and power? Money talks and the Vatican has it! The Vatican is the single wealthiest institution on the globe. Add to this incredible wealth over one billion followers strategically located in all the countries of the world, enormous political power and a leader that is loved, respected and feared by the world. Get the picture? The true evangelical believers who study the Scriptures from the fifth century to the present have believed and understood this from the book of the Revelation. The Catholic Church will indeed play a key role in fulfilling end time prophecy. Pope John Paul II has taken on the ambitious task of bringing the people of the world together. Under his power and authority he hopes to bring peace to the world by eliminating religious intolerance through the unifying of all faiths. John Paul II has become the longest reigning pope in the twentieth century, the most traveled pope in Catholic history and has far surpassed the popularity of Pope Paul VI of Vatican II.

Unity is only achieved through compromise

It matters not which religious leaders the pope meets with, whether they be Moslems, Buddhists, Hindus, animists, Shintoists, snake worshippers, New Age mystics or Protestants, he praises them all. In June of 1998, while addressing a group of delegates seeking Catholic unity with Moslems, the Pope stated:

> *Today, dialogue between our two religions is more necessary than ever. This dialogue needs to be credible*

and marked by mutual respect, knowledge and acceptance. There remains a spiritual bond which unites us and which we must strive to recognize and develop. [12]

The key word here is acceptance. Can there be any doubt what spirit is bonding them together?

Later in the same month, during the Week of Prayer for Christian Unity, John Paul II said:

I gladly take this opportunity to call the attention of all believers to the ecumenical commitment that marked the Second Vatican Council. The Council rightly defined the division among Christians as a "scandal" that "openly contradicts the will of Christ." The Council Fathers felt the need to beg pardon of God and of their brethren for the sins committed against unity. They urged Catholics to take an active and intelligent part in the work of ecumenism. Above all, the Council asks us to cultivate an authentic "spiritual ecumenism." May the Blessed Virgin, Mother of unity, make us feel the force of the Lord's voice to his disciples: "Behold, I stand at the door and knock" (Revelation 3:20). The Lord Jesus is calling everyone to deepen our ecumenical fervor and longing, as the third millennium swiftly approaches. May the Mother of Christ and of the Church obtain for all the baptized promptness and fidelity in responding to the Redeemer's ardent appeal. [13]

Mariology: the key to world acceptance

The image of Mary promises to play an important role in ushering in the one-world religion. Pope John Paul II has dedicated his papacy to Mary and has thus greatly influenced the world's attention to her. The twentieth century has become the age of Marian apparitions and pilgrimages. Literally tens of millions of people make pilgrimages to apparition sites every year. Apparitions are appearing in every corner of the world with apocalyptic messages of the antichrist. She proclaims that all religions are basically the same and we must all come together for peace. She offers an ecumenical gospel that can be accepted by Catholics, Moslems, Jews and Protestants. Her messages offer comfort and protection to those who pray the rosary. Roman Catholic Bishop Fulton Sheen once predicted the Virgin Mary would be instrumental in bringing the Moslems into the Roman Catholic Church. She is regarded by the Moslems as the most highly esteemed woman who ever lived because she chose to appear as an apparition in the city of Fatima, a city named after Mohammed's first daughter.

Two key Catholic figures assisting the Pope in his drive for ecumenical unity are Cardinal Edward Cassidy, president of the Pontifical Council for Promoting Christian Unity, and Catholic priest Tom Forrest who heads up Evangelization 2000. Strategic programs and events are taking place in an attempt to unite the world under the Pope by the year 2000. As you read these words, I know you are thinking it can never happen. There is no way the religions of the world are going to come together in unity by 2000. However, please remember the living Word of

God prophecies this unity and it will happen by consent or by force. True, it may not be achieved by the target date of 2000, but it will be achieved in the very near future. The stage is set.

A key historic event took place in the middle of 1998 with the signing of the "Joint Declaration on the Doctrine of Justification" by the Catholic Church and the World Lutheran Federation. The Pope called this declaration the *"gift of the Spirit of God's wisdom and an important ecumenical achievement."* [14]

The text overcomes historical differences that arose during the Protestant Reformation and revokes mutual condemnations exchanged between these two Churches. This declaration, he went on to say, "affirms that churches belonging to the World Lutheran Foundation and the Catholic Church have come to a substantial agreement on the question of justification, which has provoked so many controversies over the centuries." Pope John Paul II expressed hope that this might *"strengthen the declared objective of achieving full visible unity."* [15]

Another event of ecumenical importance involving the Catholic Church was the joint declaration between John Paul II and the Ecumenical Patriarch of Constantinople, Bartholomew I. The two leaders agreed to carry out a common pilgrimage toward the Great Jubilee.

At the personal request of Pope John Paul II, a series of initiatives are being considered by the Vatican in which different Christian churches could participate in important events to be held during the Great Jubilee of the year 2000. According to the official magazine of the Jubilee, *Tertium Millenium*, plans are being considered to proclaim a series of "New Martyrs." This is an unprecedented step of also naming non-Catholic martyrs who died for their faith. Another important ecumenical event will be the opening of the Holy Door in the Basilica of St. Paul, which will inaugurate the week of prayer for the Unity of Christians scheduled for January 18 to 25, 2000.

The vision of the beasts

This will not be an easy goal to accomplish by the year 2000, but the Bible prophesies it will eventually happen. In the Revelation, John has a similar vision to that of Daniel. He sees first a beast coming out of the sea which is described as the antichrist. He then sees a second beast coming out of the earth which is described as being the third member of the UNHOLY TRINITY, the false prophet.

For hundreds of years, evangelical believers read and understood the 17th and 18th chapters of Revelation to be speaking symbolically of the Catholic Church. The institution of the Catholic Church appears to be the religious vehicle which will be used by the antichrist to facilitate his control of the world's population. It will be joined by lifeless religions and apostate evangelicals the world over who have ignored or abandoned the truth of Scripture. Why would believers understand this in the text written by John on the Isle of Patmos around A.D. 90?

Constantine and the Cross

After the crucifixion and resurrection of Jesus, the disciples were empowered by the Holy Spirit on the Day of Pentecost. From that moment forward they began to fulfill the great commission given to them by the Lord Jesus Christ just prior to His ascension into heaven from the Mount of Olives:

> *Then Jesus came to them and said, "All authority in heaven and on earth has been given to me. Therefore go and make disciples of all nations, baptizing them in the name of the Father and of the Son and of the Holy Spirit, and teaching them to obey everything I have commanded you. And surely I am with you always, to the very end of the age."*
>
> Matthew 28:18-20

The book of Acts, as well as the letters of Paul, Peter and John confirm the evangelistic zeal with which the followers of Jesus lived their day-to-day lives. The result of the fact that Jesus was always on the lips of His followers was multitudes of thousands abandoning paganism and committing themselves to follow Jesus. Yes, there were persecutions. In fact, history records the excruciating deaths of thousands who chose to die at the hands of the zealous, misguided Jews and the emperor-worshipping Romans. Yet the Church grew and Christianity was here to stay. It couldn't be stamped out, snubbed or stopped! Enter Constantine. In the year A.D. 312, Constantine became the emperor of the Roman Empire. The stories vary depending on what book one reads but the essence is this: Constantine was going into battle against Maxentius at the Battle of Milvian Bridge. Supposedly, he saw an emblazoned cross in the sky and the words written, "In this sign conquer." He won the ensuing battle. Then, in 313, he issued the Edict of Milan in which he declared the Roman Empire Christian in its entirety. In other words, by decree of the emperor, pagan temples became Christian churches. Pagan priests became Christian priests. Unchanged, unregenerate people were baptized Christian. Pagan festivals became Christian holidays, etc. There was an outward acceptance of the "Christian" religion but no inward confession of sin and repentance which leads to a changed life. The persecution of genuine disciples of Jesus ceases and what appears to be a good thing ultimately was the greatest ploy of the enemy. That ploy was to get the unchanged world into the Church so that the powerful message of a changed life is diminished.

The front door to the Dark Ages

Out of this event the Catholic, or universal, as the word means, Church is birthed in the late 4th century A.D. It was this unregenerate religious system which took the world into the so-called Dark Ages, dark because the light of the Word of God was forbidden to the average person. Psalm 119:105 says, "*Your word is a lamp to my feet and a light for my path.*" Without the light of the Word of God, spiritual darkness enveloped the world. Bibles were in some cases burned and in other cases chained to pulpits. The average person did not have ready access to the

Scriptures. Superstition and tradition became the hallmarks of the Church. Make no mistake, there were always born-again believers who personally knew Jesus as Lord and Savior. However, they were intensely sought out and persecuted for their faith. Why? Because they would not agree to a religion of salvation by works with a continual sacrificing of Jesus who died once for all and said, "The just shall live by faith." This ultimately became the cry of men known as the reformers who one by one went to their excruciating deaths, refusing to submit to the Catholic creeds. Men like John Wycliffe in the 14th century, John Huss in the 15th century, and Martin Luther, John Calvin, John Knox and others in the 16th century and onwards. Men whose cry became "*Sola Scriptura,*" Scripture only, as opposed to man's traditions!

It is this brand of Christianity which today claims some 60 percent of Americans and countless other millions the world over, and yet is still largely unchanged. Out of this anemic, works-oriented religion of deception, the right-hand man of the antichrist will emerge to give credibility and validity to his plan.

Let's examine what the Bible says about this man from Revelation 13.

- *He will be a deceiver in that he will behave as a lamb, but speak like a dragon.*
- *He will force the inhabitants of the earth to worship the antichrist.*
- *He will be a miracle worker and will seemingly resurrect the wounded antichrist.*
- *He will order an image of the first beast, the antichrist, to be set up on a wing of the rebuilt temple.*
- *He will order the execution of any and all who do not cooperate.*
- *He will force everyone to take a mark either in their forehead or on their right hand and without this mark one will not be able to survive.*

Is Pope John Paul II the False Prophet? I do not know, but even if he isn't, what about the next Pope?

The office of the Papacy is a prime place to see the false prophet emerge. No other religion has an infallible head that condemns its people when they refuse to believe and obey its infallible dogmas. Catholic popes have wielded tremendous power throughout the centuries, even displacing kings and government leaders who refused to cooperate with the Vatican. There is no other religious figure on the scene today that comes close to possessing the authority, power and persuasion of the Pope.

The one-world religion will include many apostates who have departed from the faith they once professed. The Roman Catholic Church has been in apostasy for hundreds of years. Their departure from the true faith began when they started drifting away from the authority of God's Word and established an authority of their own called Tradition. Jude describes apostates as . . .

> *... godless men, who change the grace of our God into a license for immorality and deny Jesus Christ our only Sovereign and Lord* (Jude 4).

Could Jude be describing Catholics who pervert the grace of God by teaching that indulgences can remit temporal punishment for sin? Or could he be describing Catholics and liberal Protestants that deny the finished work of our all-sufficient Savior? It is these apostates who will lead people away from "the faith which was once for all delivered to the saints." They will not be led away into atheism or Buddhism but to a false Christianity that promotes a false gospel and leaves its people with a false hope of salvation. This false Christianity will produce false Christians who will one day worship the false Christ.

As we study Church history and survey the Church scene of today, we begin to see what the apostle John saw as he recorded Revelation 17 and 18. The central figure in these two chapters is a "woman" riding the beast. The woman clearly represents a world religion and has distinct characteristics that closely resemble the Roman Catholic Church. The religion is located in a city which sits on seven hills. For centuries the Catholic Church has been headquartered in Rome, a city built on seven hills.

Catholics and Protestants are uniting under the banner of Evangelism AD 2000, with an announced goal of evangelizing the world by the year 2000. They want to present Jesus with the gift of a "Christianized" world when He returns. This movement calls for all Christians to forget their theological differences and proclaim the gospel to non-Christians.

Other calls for false unity

Another movement that calls for unity between Catholics and evangelicals is led by Father John Neuhaus and Chuck Colson of Prison Fellowship. Many highly visible evangelicals signed an accord in March of 1994, called Evangelicals and Catholics Together (ECT). This accord was followed up with another one in October 1997, called The Gift of Salvation (ECT II) where Catholics and Evangelicals stated "we affirm our unity in the gospel that we have here professed." To come to this affirmation, they indeed had to forget their theological differences. The Catholic gospel is a gospel of faith plus works, where salvation is dispensed piecemeal through the sacraments, and where the work of Christ's redemption is carried on through the daily sacrifice of Jesus on Catholic altars. The gospel they have agreed upon is another gospel and really no gospel at all. It is a compromised gospel void of its power to save (Romans 1:16). As this false gospel is proclaimed throughout the world, those who believe it will end up being a gift to satan rather than to Christ.

We are not living in the Age of Aquarius. We are living in the age of apostasy! Biblical Christianity is being redefined, and repentance that brings a changed life is being replaced by an old religion with a new name, the New Age Movement. The New Agers' slogan is not "repent and believe upon the name of the Lord Jesus and be saved." Rather, their slogan is TOLERANCE! Robert Runcie, a former Archbishop of Canterbury said,

Christians must recognize the incompleteness of our

faith and enter a new age of mutual understanding whereby we acknowledge the truth in all religions!

No matter how the world defines it, Jesus said: "I am the way, the truth and the life and no man comes to the Father except by me."

The momentum of our day

In our day we are witnessing the greatest move toward a one-world religion ever seen. I know it is hard for the average evangelical believer who is part of a Bible-believing, Bible-teaching church to imagine that such a thing could happen. Yet I encourage you to re-examine the letters to the seven churches of the Revelation. These seven churches located in first century Asia Minor, modern Turkey, represent seven kinds of churches in seven ages or periods of Church history. When we examine these churches, we can clearly see that the Laodicean church is the Church of the last days, the final Church. Notice how God describes this Church.

I know your deeds, that you are neither cold nor hot. I wish you were either one or the other! So, because you are lukewarm – neither hot nor cold – I am about to spit you out of my mouth. You say, "I am rich; I have acquired wealth and do not need a thing." But you do not realize that you are wretched, pitiful, poor, blind and naked.

Revelation 3:15-17

The fact is there are few ministers and churches today across America which preach the uncompromised, whole counsel of the Word of God. While church buildings abound there is a glaring absence of sound Bible teaching which is used to teach, rebuke, correct and train in righteousness. If you are a part of a fellowship where the Word of God is taught and practiced, it is unthinkable to you that less than one out of every 1,000 churches fall into this category. Today the emphasis is on building the Church. However, the problem lies in the definition of how this is done. In most cases it means compromising the gospel message which demands repentance and trust in Jesus Christ which results in a changed life. Yes, the stage is set and deception abounds. Keep your eyes on religion and you will see where the world is going, and this sign points to who is coming!

---

[11] Vatican Information Service, June 1998.

[12] *Catholic World News*, June 1998.

[13] ibid.

[14] Vatican Information Service.

[15] ibid.

6
Sign Six: The Rebuilding of the Temple in Jerusalem

The man said to me, "Son of man,
look with your eyes and hear with your ears
and pay attention to everything
I am going to show you, for that is why
you have been brought here.
Tell the house of Israel everything you see."
I saw a wall completely
surrounding the temple area.
Ezekiel 40: 4-5

And on a wing of the temple
he will set up an abomination that
causes desolation …
Daniel 9:27

I was given a reed like a measuring rod and was told, "Go and measure the temple of God and the altar, and count the worshipers there. But exclude the outer court; do not measure it, because it has been given to the Gentiles. They will trample on the holy city for 42 months …"
Revelations 11:1-2

The Jewish Temple will be rebuilt on Temple Mount in Jerusalem and the daily sacrifices will begin again. How do we know this will happen? The Bible says so! It must be rebuilt in order for the false prophet to order an image of the antichrist erected on a wing of the Temple and demand that everyone worship him. Further we learn from Daniel:

> *From the time that the daily sacrifice is abolished and the abomination that causes desolation is set up, there will be 1,290 days.*
>
> Daniel 12:11

The Temple scenario

The Scriptures reveal that shortly after the Rapture of the true believers, the antichrist will appear on the scene as the man of the hour. He will be recommended and approved by the then pope as well as religious leaders the world over. Strangely enough, after the initial shock of the disappearance of millions, things will settle and begin to resemble some sort of normalcy. Humanity has proven time and time again to be incredibly strong and resilient. The first three and one-half years will bring the appearance of world peace. The revived form of the ancient Roman Empire will enter into a peace treaty with Israel negotiated by the antichrist. This will resolve the Middle East problem and will give Israel permission to rebuild their Temple, and they will quickly do just that. At the same time this new charismatic world leader will negotiate peace in the remaining areas of unrest. Perhaps his premise will be, since multitudes are missing, we must now put aside our differences in order to ensure our own survival.

Whatever he proposes will be accepted and the world will be at peace. However, the real strategy is being worked out behind the scenes. On the surface things appear as normal and peaceful as possible in light of the circumstances. Yet plans are being made which will change everything. Exactly 1,260 days, or three and one-half years after the signing of the treaty with Israel, everything changes. Yes, the Temple is rebuilt and Temple sacrifice is reinstituted, but then the unexpected happens. The antichrist breaks the covenant. The false prophet orders an image, perhaps a hologram of the antichrist, to be erected on a wing of the Temple. He further orders every person must worship the antichrist as god. The remaining population of the world will already have received a mark or number for identity purposes. This number may have been required as the only way to distinguish humans from alien beings who could be among us. Sounds silly doesn't it? Yet remember, millions have vanished! Just try to explain that. It will be this number or mark, on either the right hand or the forehead, which will allow one to exist. Of course, with Biometrics, retina scans, implanted microchips and more, this is a small task to accomplish but it will take some time. It will take three and one-half years to be exact.

The longing for the Temple

For the past 2,000 years the Jewish people have mourned the destruction of the Temple in Jerusalem.

Even today, Orthodox Jews recite a petition three times daily for the restoration of the Temple. During the Jewish wedding ceremony, the Temple is remembered. At the ceremony's conclusion, the groom breaks a glass goblet the couple has shared. The rabbis have stated that this is done as a sign of solidarity with the Jewish community in mourning for the Temple. However, the greatest display of affection for the Temple is observed annually. Each year on the anniversary of the destruction of the Temple there is a solemn day of mourning which is observed. The ninth day of the Jewish month of Av (our July/August) both the first Temple and the second was destroyed. The First Temple, constructed by King Solomon, stood for 374 years until the Babylonians destroyed it in 586 B.C. The Second Temple, rebuilt under the leadership of Zerubbabel and Ezra, later enlarged and beautified by Herod the Great, towered over Jerusalem for 586 years until its destruction at the hands of the Roman tenth legion in A.D. 70.

Since A.D. 70, it has been the desire of the Jewish people to rebuild their Temple. This has been especially true since their return to their land in 1948. However, the desire escalated in June 1967, when the Israelis captured the Old City of Jerusalem and the 35 acres known as Temple Mount. From that day to this, there has been a heightened desire to once again construct their temple on the site where it stood until its destruction in A.D. 70.

The rebuilders today

In Jerusalem today, there is a group of Jewish Zealots led by Rabbi Chaim Richmond and Gershon Salomon of the Temple Institute. They call themselves the Temple Mount Faithful. It is their passion to see the temple rebuilt and to re-institute the sacrificial system once again. The Bible says this will happen in the final seven years of Daniel's 70th week. The sacrificial system will be reinstituted only to be stopped at the three and one-half-year point by the antichrist as he invalidates his treaty of peace with Israel and turns on her with intense persecution that will make the Holocaust look like a day at the beach!

Why is this soon-to-transpire event of prophetic importance to us? This is one more of the signs which point to the second coming of Christ and which reminds us of the nearness of the Rapture. It is this desire to rebuild the Temple on the part of so many in the world that directs our attention once again to Israel and the Middle East.

To build or not to build

I think it is important to note that while many religious Jews desire to see the Temple rebuilt, others are not the least bit interested. Many Jews believe the Temple is a relic of the past and they can get along just fine without it. On the other side, there are those who feel the Jewish world, and all humanity for that matter, are living below God's intended level of spiritual awareness. They claim that the reason for this is because of the absence of the Shekinah or Divine Presence of God from the world. On one of my visits to the Temple Institute, located in the Old City of Jerusalem, our group met with Rabbi Richmond. I had been privileged to speak with him privately on many occasions previously. However, on this occasion, he made a statement during our meeting I thought was most interesting. He said, "The Shekinah is brought about only through the Temple." He went on to add, "In terms of our mission as a people, we cannot in any way reach our spiritual status without the Temple."

Today, Jews are denied access to the Temple Mount with regard to praying and conducting religious services. However, even as I write, word has been received that during the coming commemoration of Tisha B'Av (9th of Av), the Temple Mount Faithful in Jerusalem are planning an awareness program to heighten interest and understanding among both Christians and Jews. Their agenda is stated as follows:

> *We shall concentrate all our efforts so that on this day every Israeli will be with us on Temple Mount. We*

> *shall pray together with them for the rebuilding of the Temple and Jerusalem. We shall also march in the streets of the Old City and around all the gates of the Temple Mount especially the Golden Gate in the eastern wall of the Temple Mount. This gate expresses very old beliefs and traditions that the Messiah will enter the Temple through it. After the Six Day War one of the followers of the movement wrote in big blue letters on this gate — "Mashiach will come soon." This will be a very special and exciting event, and we invite all of our friends to come to Israel and take part in it.* [16]

However, the primary reason the Temple will be reconstructed is not because Jewish zealots want it rebuilt, but because the antichrist himself wants it built. That's right: it is the antichrist who intends to use the Temple for his own self-serving means. This will be satan's final attempt to force the inhabitants of the world to pay him homage and worship him as God!

Spiritual versus physical

Little do Gershon Salomon, Rabbi Richmond, and the thousands who are planning for this to take place, know that they are actually preparing the very articles which will eventually be used by satan incarnate, the antichrist. Make no mistake, there will be a literal physical stone and mortar Temple rebuilt in Jerusalem. This teaching is not to be spiritualized and understood as a spiritual temple. One cannot place an image on a wing of a spiritual temple and demand all the world worship it, nor can one stop the sacrificing of animals in a spiritual temple. The Temple is coming!

In that same place where the armies of Babylon trampled over the sacred precincts, those walls of worship will be raised again. On the same soil that knew the iron heel of Rome's legions crushing the Herodian Temple, there will be built again the ramparts and turrets of a mighty house of worship. You could just as soon keep the sun from rising in the east, or the tides from ebbing and flowing, as you could stop the will of God. It will be built.

[16] *The Messianic Times*, Vol. Nine, No. Two, Summer 1998

7
Sign Seven: The Rage and Retribution of Armageddon

Then they gathered the kings together to

the place that in Hebrew is called Armageddon.

Revelation 16:16

Recently I saw the movie entitled *Armageddon*. In this action-packed, nail-biting thriller the hero, played by Bruce Willis, saves the world from utter annihilation. (He supposedly was paid 60 million dollars to do this; now that's motivation.) In the movie a giant meteor is on a collision course with planet earth. If this meteor hits, it will destroy every living thing. Of course, it never makes it because our hero detonates a nuclear bomb which blows him and the giant meteor into billions of small harmless particles (wonder what happens to the $60 million?). These pieces end up being burned up upon entry into the earth's gravitational field. Ho hum, just another blockbuster thriller with a safe and happy ending.

The earth dodges destruction once again and humanity is seemingly indestructible. But is this what Armageddon is really about? The word "armageddon" has become synonymous with destruction, and rightly so. But where does the word come from and why is it always associated with death and destruction? To answer this we must go to the Word.

Will the world be destroyed?

The most awesome event, resulting in the greatest devastation and destruction the world has known or ever will know, is not a battle or war at all. Rather it is a three and one-half year military campaign. However, there is coming a time when the world will in fact almost be destroyed. This fact is worthy of our interest and understanding. Notice the word "almost." We hear on a daily basis the crisis facing our world. There is the possibility of nuclear war initiated by man. There is the highly-publicized threat of mankind's ecological destruction resulting in harmful cancer-causing rays from the sun. Polluted and disease-infested water abounds. Gas and chemical-laden air fills the atmosphere so thickly that one can cut it with a knife. These are only a few of the possibilities which exist that could result in earth's demise by mankind. On the other hand, there are very real threats of earth's colliding with pieces of rock flying through the air at thousands of miles per hour which would wreak havoc, to say the least, and which man has absolutely no control over whatsoever. So, will the world be destroyed? The world will be destroyed, but not by man, nor by asteroids, but by God himself in the end. It will not, however, happen at Armageddon.

The final sign of the second coming of Christ has to do with God's dealing in judgment with the nations and peoples of the world with regard to three specific areas:

- *Their persecution of Israel (Joel 3:2).*
- *Their sinfulness (Rev. 19:15).*
- *Their godlessness (Rev.16:9).*

Ancient Megiddo: Ominous sign of the future

There is a very real geographically locatable spot in Israel known throughout the ages as Har Megiddo, or the hill of Megiddo, hence the name *Armageddon*. Megiddo overlooks the famous Jezreel Valley, also known as the Plain of Esdraelon and the bread basket of the Middle East. Megiddo lies in ruins today but it had a rich and eventful history. Archaeologists have uncovered the remains of some twenty different levels of civilization at this ancient site. The city lies along one of the most important ancient trade routes in the world known as the Via Maris, or the Way of the Sea. It was a fortified city strategically built to control travel along this trade route. One of Israel's judges, Deborah, and her aid, Barak, fought against Sisera and the Canaanites in the same region (Judges 4-5). Gideon defeated the Midianites there (Judges 7). King Saul was slain in battle against the Philistines (1 Samuel 31:8). King Solomon captured the city and made it one of his chariot cities around 975 B.C. Napoleon described the valley of Armageddon as the greatest natural battlefield in all the world. He said, "All the armies of the world could maneuver here." In commenting on this location, Vincent says:

> *Megiddo was in the plain of Esdraelon, "which has been a chosen place for encampment in every contest carried on in Palestine from the days of Nabuchodonozor, King of Assyria, unto the disastrous march of*

> *Napoleon Bonaparte from Egypt into Syria. Jews, Gentiles, Saracens, Christian crusaders and anti-Christian Frenchmen; Egyptians, Persians, Druses, Turks, and Arabs, warriors of every nation that is under heaven, have pitched their tents on the plains of Esdraelon, and have beheld the banners of their nation wet with the dews of Tabor and Hermon.* [17]

While Megiddo has always been associated with the end-times' battle, "*the battle of that great day of God Almighty*" (Rev. 16:14), Scripture teaches something very different. First, the Battle of Armageddon is not a battle but a series of military campaigns. The word translated "battle" is the Greek word *polemos*, which means war or campaign. This carries with it the idea of a series of conflicts as opposed to a specific battle. For example, the Battle of the Bulge was only one of the many battles which made up World War II. The second item worthy of our understanding is that this war or campaign will encompass the entire land of Israel, not just the Valley of Armageddon. Sims says:

> *. . . it appears from Scripture that this last great battle of the great day of God Almighty will reach far beyond Armageddon, the Valley of Megiddo. Armageddon appears to be mainly the place where the troops will gather together from the four corners of earth, and from Armageddon the battle will spread out over the entire land of Palestine. Joel speaks of the last battle being fought in the Valley of Jehoshaphat, which is close by Jerusalem, and Isaiah shows Christ coming with blood-stained garments from Edom, and Edom is south of Palestine. So the battle of Armageddon, it seems, will stretch from the Valley of Megiddo in the north of Palestine, through the Valley of Jehoshaphat, near Jerusalem, and on down to Edom at the extreme southern part of Palestine.* [18]

Revelation 14:20 also reveals that a river of blood will flow to the horses' bridles, four and one-half feet deep, for 1,600 stadia, or 200 miles, which clearly encompasses all of modern-day Israel with the exception of the southern Negev or desert.

The scenario unfolds

The Scriptures give a broad overview of how God will eventually pour out His wrath upon an unbelieving, humanistic, Christ-rejecting world. It is not a pretty picture. It appears the antichrist will be accepted by all during the first three and one-half years after the signing of the peace treaty with Israel, according to Revelation 13:3. This event (the signing of the peace treaty) marks the actual beginning of the final seven years also known as Daniel's 70th week (Daniel 9:27). However, in the middle of this period he loses his popularity when the False Prophet declares that everyone must worship him as god or die (Revelation 13:15). In addition we are told in Revelation 12:7-17 that there is a great war which takes place in heaven. The fight is between God and the devil himself. Satan has always had access to heaven, and in fact accuses the saved before God. This time, God casts him out of heaven and into the earth. In his anger and wrath he turns against the Jewish people and begins to intensely persecute them for three and one-half years. His plan is to annihilate them once and for all. Satan incarnate, the antichrist, assisted by his powerful military force, moves against Israel. This brings a response from the nations of the world who finally begin to realize that, if he does it to Israel, he could do it to them. Somewhere in this time period a great army of some 200 million soldiers from an Eastern power begin to march upon Israel where the antichrist has headquartered (Revelation 9:16, 16:12). Red China has officially claimed an army of more than 200 million, the largest standing army on the globe. This movement brings up a great army from the south followed by a huge force from the north and west. All the nations of the world are converging upon Israel to fight against the antichrist and his false prophet. However, it appears something happens which causes these armies to unite together to fight against the God of heaven himself. Remember, at this juncture more than 50 percent of the remaining world's population has died from various judgments of God already poured out upon planet earth (Revelation 6:8, one-quarter die; 9:15-33, one-third of the remaining die). David penned these words recorded in the Psalms:

> *Why do the nations conspire and the peoples plot in vain? The kings of the earth take their stand and the rulers gather together against the LORD and against his Anointed One. "Let us break their chains," they say, "and throw off their fetters." The One enthroned in heaven laughs; the Lord scoffs at them. Then he rebukes them in his anger and terrifies them in his wrath, saying, "I have installed my King on Zion, my holy hill."*
>
> Psalm 2: 1-6, 9

Man in his final act of foolish defiance thinks he can destroy the God of creation. God speaks through Zechariah the prophet and says:

> *I am going to make Jerusalem a cup that sends all the surrounding peoples reeling. Judah will be besieged as well as Jerusalem. On that day, when all*

the nations of the earth are gathered against her, I will make Jerusalem an immovable rock for all the nations. All who try to move it will injure themselves.

Zechariah 12:2-3

I will gather all the nations to Jerusalem to fight against it; the city will be captured, the houses ransacked, and the women raped. Half of the city will go into exile, but the rest of the people will not be taken from the city. Then the LORD will go out and fight against those nations, as he fights in the day of battle. On that day his feet will stand on the Mount of Olives, east of Jerusalem, and the Mount of Olives will be split in two from east to west, forming a great valley, with half of the mountain moving north and half moving south. You will flee by my mountain valley, for it will extend to Azel. You will flee as you fled from the earthquake in the days of Uzziah king of Judah. Then the LORD my God will come, and all the holy ones with him.

Zechariah 14:2-5

It will be a day like no other the world has ever witnessed. The particulars of exactly how this three and one-half-year campaign comes to an end are not really all that important. What is important is the outcome: JESUS WINS, SATAN LOSES! The forces of the antichrist, along with representatives from every nation and peoples on this globe, are destroyed by the "brightness of His appearing."

The millennial reign of Christ

What follows this massive carnage? The saints of God, the returning Bride of Christ, come with the King of Kings and Lord of Lords and life as we now know it is over. It is finished! He establishes what Scripture calls His millennial reign upon earth. A 1,000 year reign of peace on this earth will be inaugurated by Christ and the saved will reign with Him:

And they sang a new song:
"You are worthy to take the scroll
and to open its seals,

because you were slain,
and with your blood you purchased men for God
from every tribe and language and people
and nation.
You have made them to be a kingdom and priests
to serve our God,
and they will reign on the earth."

Revelation 5: 9-10

Not only does the New Testament teach, but the early church also believed that Jesus would reign on the earth as King of the very planet that rejected him. Papias of Hierapolis, who heard the living voice of John, reinforced that in his own writings. Irenaeus of Lyon, the famous bishop in Gaul, eloquently taught the reign of Jesus Christ. Justin Martyr, the early Christian apologist, made it clear in his *Dialogue with Trypho,* the Jew, that Jesus would reign from Jerusalem in His own Kingdom. Victorinus of Petau who wrote the first commentary on Revelation insisted likewise that Jesus would reign. Hippolytus of Rome, Lactantius, Tertullian,

Commodianus, Methodius of Olympus and numerous other early Christian writers all took it for granted that Jesus would reign on the earth in His own Kingdom. There was no other view that even appeared in the early church until after A.D. 250. The unanimous consent of the earliest Christians embraced the reign of Jesus on this earth in a renewed form. This is a necessity to fulfill the Model Prayer. When shall it be fulfilled that God's will shall be done on earth as it is in heaven? Shall it not be when our Lord reigns unchallenged in His authority? As Irenaeus wrote so clearly, it is necessary that He reign in the very world that rejected Him.

Maranatha, even so come Lord Jesus!

---

[17] Marvin R. Vincent, *Word Studies in the New Testament, II*, p. 630

[18] A. Sims, *The Coming War and the Rise of Russia*, p. 7

It's A Wrap

Finally, be strong in the Lord
and in his mighty power.
Put on the full armor of God
so that you can take your stand
against the devil's schemes.
Ephesians 6:10-11

We are all familiar with the words of the motion picture director. After the work is done, after the plan is completed, after the participants have done their part, finally come the words, "It's a wrap!" In other words, it is finished. Everyone who has ever seen a movie knows intuitively when the end of the movie is near. There are signs, certain indicators, which clue us in to the fact that the script has been played out and now it is time to go.

The writer of a novel sits at his or her laptop and roughly sketches out the plan for the story. It must have an exciting beginning, an interest-keeping plot and a stirring ending. As one reads the story, one understands they are progressing toward the end. The signs are easily recognized.

Life, created by God Himself, has a beginning. I shall never cease to be amazed at how God creates a precious new life and brings that life into this world only to allow it to begin to die. The moment we breathe our first breath we are progressing toward our last. Someone wisely observed, "the wood of the cradle rubs against the marble of the tombstone." The end of one's life has its indicators, its signs. We tend to develop furniture disease, that is, our chest falls into our drawers. We develop the *B syndrome*: baldness, bulges, bifocals and bunions. We can recognize time is slipping away.

In our world, while we can readily agree with the above statements, we cannot seem to come to grip with the same reality as it relates to God's eternal plan for the ages. The signs surround us. The Word of God tells us how to recognize what time it is. Yet, for the most part, we plunge ahead as though this movie, this novel, our life, this world, has no end.

Now what?

So, what are we to do? I had hoped you would be asking yourself this question, because I have a few suggestions.

First, you come to grips with the reality we are, in fact, running out of time. You will want to make certain you know, not just know about, the person of

Jesus Christ as the Savior and Lord of your life. Most people today say they believe in God. Yet their lives do not substantiate this as fact. The problem has to do with one's understanding and definition of the word "believe." The Bible says the devil "believes" in God (James 2:19), but I can assure you he isn't going to heaven. What does it mean to "believe" in Jesus, since the Scriptures teach that the only way to be rightly related to God is through belief in Jesus as the Christ (Romans 10:9-10)? Perhaps the best way to define the word "believe" is by an illustration.

Walking a tightrope

Suppose I was a tight rope walker and you saw me perform. You were satisfied I could walk a tightrope. I then posed a question, "Do you believe I can walk the tightrope?"

You would naturally say, "Yes, I believe you can walk the tightrope."

However, if I said to you, "If you believe I can walk the rope, get on my back and let me take you for a walk."

Whoa! Wait a minute! Now we are talking about something entirely different. We are talking about my believing to the degree where action is taken. That's it. Now you are getting it. To believe is not to utter a word or phrase with your lips. Rather to believe demands action on one's part. It means to demonstrate through action. To believe in Jesus means I trust in Him and Him alone for my salvation. In addition, I know Him and there is a relationship with God. That belief is demonstrated daily in my life by how I live. Please be certain you know God, not just know about Him, but know Him through the living Lord Jesus Christ.

Secondly, you will want to be certain that everyone you love and care about knows the "Good News" of Jesus. There is no way we can keep the news of forgiveness and restoration to ourselves. We want to give it away to our loved ones, even if they are not receptive. This is often the case. It is often said that the hardest people to talk to about Jesus are our loved ones. Why? Because they know us and they know we aren't perfect. In addition, they fail to understand that when we were saved we didn't get perfect, we got forgiven. It's hard for unsaved folks to realize that as a follower of Jesus our lives are "under construction." In our obedience, God is working to shape us into the image of Jesus, and that task will take the rest of our earthly lives. But let me hasten to add, if you do not care for the soul of your loved one, it is doubtful anyone else will. Therefore, I believe we have the responsibility to do all within our power under the anointing of God's Holy Spirit to reach those we love.

Prayer and the armor of God

I want to suggest how to effectively pray for our loved ones. First, we must understand there is a spiritual battle being fought over the souls of all people. If you do not believe every person who dies without Jesus steps into a literal hell, you will never be a true prayer warrior. Once we accept this truth, we then begin to understand what the Scriptures mean:

> *For though we live in the world, we do not wage war as the world does. The weapons we fight with are not the weapons of the world. On the contrary, they have divine power to demolish strongholds. We demolish arguments and every pretension that sets itself up against the knowledge of God, and we take captive every thought to make it obedient to Christ.*
>
> 2 Corinthians 10:3-5

Here we are told that we have weapons with which to fight, but that they are unconventional. They are spiritual weapons. These spiritual weapons are used to virtually tear down strongholds which have been built up in the lives of our loved ones. What are strongholds and how are they torn down? Strongholds are those areas of our lives where we have allowed the devil to gain access. In many cases, these areas are pride, sexual addiction, fantasies, love for material things, quest for fame, acceptance or any number of things. God says these strongholds keep one from coming to Jesus. However, we can fight against these and demolish them through intercessory prayer. This is the weapon of our faith against which no person can stand, including the demons of hell.

How do we fight the devil? The answer to this is also found in the Scriptures:

> *Finally, be strong in the Lord and in his mighty power. Put on the full armor of God so that you can take your stand against the devil's schemes. For our struggle is not against flesh and blood, but against the rulers, against the authorities, against the powers of this dark world and against the spiritual forces of evil in the heavenly realms. Therefore put on the full armor of God, so that when the day of evil comes, you may be able to stand your ground, and after you have done everything, to stand. Stand firm then, with the belt of truth buckled around your waist, with the breastplate of righteousness in place, and with your feet fitted with the readiness that comes from the gospel of peace. In addition to all this, take*

up the shield of faith, with which you can extinguish all the flaming arrows of the evil one. Take the helmet of salvation and the sword of the Spirit, which is the word of God. And pray in the Spirit on all occasions with all kinds of prayers and requests. With this in mind, be alert and always keep on praying for all the saints.

Ephesians 6:10-18

Here we learn that the warfare is prayer. The enemy is the devil. The objective is the stronghold in one's life. The strategy for victory is the armor of God. We must first be willing to fight. That is, we must care enough to engage the enemy. Many simply do not have the will, the resolve to fight. We then must clothe ourselves with the armor of God. This is difficult and here's why. We cannot put on the armor of God unless we ourselves are spiritually clean before God. This means we must be confessed up. Scripture says, "*If we confess our sins, he is faithful and just and will forgive us our sins and purify us from all unrighteousness*" (1 John 1:9). God cannot fight through a dirty vessel. Once we are clean, we can then go to battle clothed in truth. The first step is to ask God to reveal to us the particular stronghold which is keeping our loved one from Him. If we are serious about this and seek an answer from God, He will speak to our heart and supernaturally reveal the stronghold to us. Once this is identified, we then begin to apply scriptural truth against it. That is, we search for Scripture to use against the stronghold and we pray this in behalf of our loved one. For example, if God reveals that a spirit of pride is the main stronghold, we can pray the following:

Dear Lord,

Your word says you hate pride and arrogance (Proverbs 8:13). That pride only breeds quarrels (Proverbs 13:10). That pride goes before destruction (Proverbs 16:18). That the cravings of a sinful man, the lust of his eyes and the boasting of what he has and does, come not from the Father but from the world (1 John 2:16). Therefore in the strong and powerful name of Jesus I tear down this barrier of pride and demand that it depart from my loved one.

This is how we use the weapon of Scripture to tear down strongholds. Will the loved one come to Jesus? He or she may not; there are no guarantees. However, once they are set free from the bondage, there is every reason to believe and claim them for the kingdom of God.

Once we are clean, once we have engaged in spiritual warfare, then it is time to boldly witness in a spirit of love. As we listen to God speak to our hearts, we will hear Him say it is time to GO. There comes a time when we must put legs to our prayers. Let me illustrate. A couple of years ago, my wife, Sandra, came to me and said she felt it was time to go and visit a certain member of her family who lived out of state. She had been engaging in intercessory prayer for some months and now God said GO. She went, not knowing how she would be received, but in obedience and love. She phoned me within twenty-four hours to share the exciting news of how her loved one had trusted Christ and been born again. It doesn't always work like this, but in the last thirty-eight months we have now seen twenty-five (as of this writing) of our unsaved loved ones accept Jesus as their Lord and Savior. Why do we pray? Why do we go? Because Jesus is coming and time is running out.

The day, the hour, when?

The year was 1840 and William Miller, a New York farmer turned Baptist preacher, was preaching that Jesus was coming soon. He went so far as to begin to teach that he knew when Jesus was coming again. It seems that preacher Miller had read Daniel 8:14 and interpreted the statement regarding 2,300 evenings and mornings to be 2,300 years. He then concluded that Christ would return sometime between March 21, 1843, and March 21, 1844.

To preacher Miller's credit, he did not pinpoint a precise day or hour, but did narrow it down to a twelve-month window. There were many who accepted Miller's teaching and became enthusiastic followers of this teaching. Sadly enough, March 21, 1844, came and went and Jesus did not come as Miller had predicted. Stories abound about how some of the Millerites quit their jobs and donned white robes. Further, they ascended up the mountains and awaited the coming of Jesus, only to be sadly disappointed. Samuel Snow, however, a follower of Miller's teaching, injected new life into this when he suggested there had been an error in calculating and the real date would now be October 22, 1844. October 22, 1844, came and went and this event has now become known as THE GREAT DISAPPOINTMENT of 1844. Many went away completely disillusioned. Some abandoned the faith and returned to lives of sin while others remained faithful to Christ and realized, whether He returned physically in their lifetime or not, they would someday be with Him for He would come for them in death.

William Miller is not alone. Many throughout

the last 2,000 years have sought to announce the return of Jesus. Because of this, many have decided that they want no part of Bible prophecy and have chosen to ignore this wealth of vital information. How sad! I believe these prophetic truths are the single greatest motivational truths contained in the Holy Scriptures. Prophecy motivates us to be holy, to pray, to witness, to give, to serve and to strive to be all Christ wants us to be, because He is coming at any moment.

Yes, some have predicted and missed it. Charles H. Spurgeon asked, however, a riveting question: "Shall I drain the sea because there are some sharks? Shall I refuse the medicine because there is some poison?"

"Obviously not," is our answer.

Today, we have every reason to believe we are living in the final days. I believe Jesus is coming! But, whether He comes today, tomorrow, next week, next month, next year or not in my lifetime, it's okay. Why? Because whenever He comes, I will see Him, for I am His and He is mine. In the end, it's a sure thing!